Green on Blue

Green on Blue

ELLIOT ACKERMAN

DAUNT BOOKS

First published in Great Britain in 2016 by
Daunt Books
83 Marylebone High Street
London W1U 4QW

1

Copyright © 2015 Elliot Ackerman

The right of Elliot Ackerman to be identified as the author
of the Work has been asserted by him in accordance with
the Copyright, Designs and Patents Act 1988.

A CIP catalogue record for this title is available from the British Library.

ISBN 978-1-907970-79-5

Typeset by Tetragon, London
Printed and bound by T J International Ltd, Padstow, Cornwall

www.dauntbookspublishing.co.uk

For Ali and Big Cheese
who were my friends

Allah's Apostle said, 'War is deceit.'

IMAM AL-BUKHARI
AD 846

I

MANY WOULD CALL ME a dishonest man, but I've always kept faith with myself. There is an honesty in that, I think.

I am Ali's brother. We are from a village that no longer exists and our family was not large or prosperous. The war that came after the Russians but before the Americans killed our parents. Of them, I have only dim memories. There is my father's Kalashnikov hidden in a woodpile by the door, him cleaning it, working oiled rags on its parts, and the smell of gunmetal and feeling safe. There is my mother's secret, the one she shared with me. Once a month she'd count out my father's earnings from fighting in the mountains or farming. She'd send me and Ali from our village, Sperkai, to the large bazaar in Orgun, a two-day walk. The Orgun bazaar sold everything: fine cooking oils and spices, candles to light our home and fabrics to repair our clothes. My mother always entrusted me with a special purchase. Before we left, she would press an extra coin in my hand, one she'd stolen from my father. Among the crowded stalls of the bazaar, I would slip away from my brother's watchful eye and buy her a pack of cigarettes, a vice forbidden to a woman.

When we returned home, I would place the pack in her hiding spot – the birchwood cradle where she'd rocked Ali and

3

me as infants. Our mud-walled house was small, two thatch-roofed rooms with a courtyard between them. The cradle was kept in the room I shared with Ali. My mother would never get rid of the cradle. It was the one thing that was truly hers. At night, after we'd returned from the bazaar, she'd sneak into our room, her small, sandalled feet gliding across the carpets that lined the dirt floor. Her hand would cup a candle, its smothered light casting shadows on her young face, ageing her. Her eyes, one brown and the other green, a miracle or defect of birth, shifted about the room. Carefully she would lean over the cradle, as she'd done before taking us to nurse. She would run her fingers between the blankets that once swaddled my brother and me and, finding the pack I'd left her, she'd step into the courtyard. And I'd fall back asleep to the faint smell of her tobacco just past my door.

This secret made me feel close to my mother. In the years since, I've wondered why she entrusted me with it. At times, I've thought it was because I was her favourite. But this isn't why. The truth is, she recognised in me her own ability to deceive.

Like most men, my father farmed a small plot. He understood the complexity of modest tasks – how to tap the ever shifting waters of an underground karez, how to irrigate a field with that water, how to place a boulder at the curve of a furrow so the turning flow would not erode the bend. He taught these lessons to me and Ali. We grew, working by his side, our land binding us together, sure as blood.

In the warm months, my father would head to the mountains, to fight. His group operated under the Haqqanis, and later joined Hezb-e-Islami, but loyalties shifted often. My brother told me that when my father was killed, his group was again with the Haqqanis but now they all served under the Taliban. For a boy these things meant little. Sometimes I wonder how much they matter even to a man.

When I last saw my parents it was summer. Against the Taliban's orders, my father's group had returned home early. They'd disobeyed their commanders after being told to extort taxes along a certain road. At the time, I understood none of this. On that last morning, my father slept late and my mother prepared breakfast in the courtyard. Ali and I had no work to do on our land, and we grew tired of waiting for my father to wake. Our mother grew tired of restless boys, and she shooed us off to gather pine nuts for the meal. We wandered away from the village towards the tall trees lining a ridge. Ali climbed their thick trunks and shook their branches. I gathered the cones that fell, cracking them open between two rocks and picking the nuts from each.

That year, Ali had grown strong enough to climb onto the highest branches. His long arms would grasp above him as he took powerfully assured steps up the tree, without pausing. He'd only stop when no branches remained to take him higher. When I climbed, I'd test each branch, tugging it to ensure it could hold my weight.

He was about to turn thirteen and would be a boy for only a short while longer. Each year, our mother would buy a bolt of fabric and make one new set of clothes. Ali would get the new set and I'd get his hand-me-down. He was always larger than me, and my clothes never fit.

We both had little education. When my mother was a girl, she'd learned to read and write in a school built by the Russians. She taught us how, but nothing more. My father had never been to school. He'd fought the Russians instead. Now that Ali was old enough to travel on his own, my father planned to send him to the madrassa in Orgun.

What will you learn there? I asked, my head tilted back, staring up at Ali among the pine branches.

I don't know, he said. If I did, I would not have to learn it.

You leave in the autumn? I asked.

Yes, Aziz, but you'll see me when you come to the bazaar. And in two years, when you're old enough, maybe you'll join me.

Ali shook a high branch and more cones fell around me. I broke them against the rocks. My pockets were nearly filled with nuts when I heard the sound of an engine in the distance. Ali waved after me and I climbed into the branches with him.

What I saw next I didn't understand. To remember it is like being on a high trail in the fog, feeling but not seeing the mountains around you. First there was the dust of people running. Behind the dust was a large flatbed truck and many smaller ones. They pushed the villagers as a broom cleans the streets. A shipping container lay on the bed of the large truck. Amid the dust and the heat, I saw men with guns. The men looked like my father but they began to shoot the villagers who ran.

I tried to climb down from the tree, but Ali held me to its trunk. We hid among the branches. A thought came to me again and again: my father has a rifle too, these men must know my father. Soon the shooting finished. The living and dead were locked together inside the container. I looked for my father but saw him nowhere. The gunmen walked from home to home. They lit the thatched roofs on fire. Still, I told myself not to worry. My father had a rifle. No harm could come to him.

All that day the fires burned. The wind changed and we choked on the smoke from our home. We had no water. The flames receded in the night, but this gave us little relief. Hungry and thirsty, we returned to our village in the morning. The truck and container were gone. Sperkai was empty and smouldering.

In our home, the carpets were little more than ash brushed across a dirt floor. My mother's cradle had collapsed into a pile of charred sticks. But my father's Kalashnikov lay hidden by the door, mixed with the woodpile's embers. I reached for the damaged rifle. Ali swatted my hand away. He had no interest in it.

This is no longer our home, he said.

I clutched my hand to my chest. It stung from where Ali had struck me. I opened my mouth to speak, but my throat filled with the sorrow of all I'd lost. I swallowed, then asked: Where will we go?

You'll come with me, he answered as though he were a destination.

We travelled the familiar road to Orgun. In the city, we hoped to find work and perhaps some news of our parents. Each day we begged our meals in the streets. Cars sped by us. Grey buildings rose several storeys high, a stream of people passing in and out of them. We crouched in the doorways. As crowded as Orgun was, it might as well have been deserted. We never saw the same face twice. Those who looked at us did so with pity, as if we were doomed boys. Ali was nearly a man, but having no family made him a boy.

Once, in Sperkai, an older child had split my lip in a fight. When my father saw this, he took me to the boy's home. Standing at their front gate, he demanded that the father take a lash to his son. The man refused and my father didn't ask twice. He struck the man in the face, splitting his lip just as his son had split mine. Before the man could get back to his feet my father left, the matter settled. On the walk home, my father spoke to me of badal, revenge. He told me how a man, a Pashtun man, had an obligation to take badal when his nang, his honour, was challenged. In Orgun, every stranger's glance made me ache for a time when my father might return and take badal against those who'd pitied his sons.

Ali and I would beg during the days. At night we would leave Orgun and cross the high desert plain to the low hills that surrounded the city. There we would rest with the other orphans. Among them, we'd share a crack in the earth or the embers of a spent fire, our shadows mixing as we slept. Some stayed for a night or two, never to be seen again, others stayed for years. Ali warned me against befriending these boys. He didn't trust anyone as poor as us.

We lived like this for two winters.

*

One night as we left Orgun, it began to snow. Ali and I stumbled across the barren plain. Dust turned to mud in the storm. The snow gathered on the earth and on our shoes and clothes. Our bodies melted the snow and we became wet. Around us, the storm and the darkness blew neither white nor black, just empty. Soon we were lost. On the plain, there was no fold in the earth or clump of trees to protect us. Far off, we saw a square shadow. We staggered towards it, and pulled open the rusted hinges of some metal doors, and climbed inside. Outside the cold had cut into us, but inside the cold came differently, it stuck. Ali struck a match. The shelter appeared empty, but then, in the corner, I saw rags, pieces of torn clothing. I gathered them and my brother built a weak fire. The flames danced against the walls. Long claw marks ran down the walls, to the steel of the seams. At the seams were nicks and dents, places where the metal had been pulled up. The fire went out. The storm heaved outside. In the dark I sat against Ali and shook.

In the morning I woke up alone. The door was cracked open and it showed a sliver of perfect blue. Outside, Ali sat on his knees in the snow. The shelter was a shipping container. I crouched beside him.

Shall we go back to Orgun? I asked.

Ali spoke in a quiet voice as he looked at the far-off hills: Remember the tower?

I turned my eyes to where he was looking. A radio tower stood atop one of the hills. We had seen the same tower from our home in Sperkai. At night it flashed a red light. Our father had a story about that tower and a silver ring he wore, set with a chip of ruby. He used to tell us how the stone was made of the tower's light, and how when he was younger he'd climbed the steel scaffolding and stolen it. I can't remember when I stopped believing the story, but by that morning I no longer did. My father had promised the ring to Ali when he was grown. Ali had once pestered my father about the ring, asking how much longer he would have to wait. My father had told him: When you aren't a boy who whines about a ring then you'll have it.

Now Ali held up his hand to me. I saw he wore the small ruby on his thumb.

Where did you get that? I asked, feeling hope and fear.

I found it in the corner, answered Ali.

But he—

He never would have left the ring, said Ali sharply.

I sat next to my brother in the snow. I imagined one of the men who'd come to our village that day, pulling the ring from our father's finger only to later forget it – or, worse, discard it as junk. I thought of my father's hands. They'd always been strong – strong enough to claw marks into the container's side.

Ali looked at me, and in the space between breaths his eyes filled and then dried like a quick tide.

What now? I asked.

My brother stood and said: I think this is the season's last snow.

He used to go to the mountains after the last snow, I answered, and moved beside him.

Yes, said Ali, his voice like a whisper. I will do better for you, Aziz.

In the summer he figured a way.

*

It started with a wheelbarrow. Ali found it in a ravine and began to haul me around Orgun in it. Its empty front tyre flapped against the dust and announced our arrival with every bump. I rode in the scoop and played the cripple. I'd droop my arms, hide my legs beneath a canvas sack as if I had none, and breathe heavily through an open mouth. Along the streets Ali would shout: Zakat for my brother! Charity for my poor cripple of a brother!

Five times a day, after the faithful finished namaz, Ali would wheel me to one of the city's mosques. The mullahs often passed out scraps of food, some naan or a bowl of plain rice. The wealthy pray less than the poor, so we begged for change in the bazaar. Here Ali would struggle to hold the wheelbarrow upright as the crowds pressed against it. Beside the heaps of scrap metal, stacks of lumber, and sacks of pistachios and pomegranates, merchants shouted their prices into the street. Ali's voice mixed with the merchants as he cried out for zakat, and I slumped in the wheelbarrow playing my part. Mostly we were ignored or shooed away, but from time to time a coin would be pressed into my brother's palm just as my mother once pressed one into mine.

After a few hours' begging, my legs would begin to ache. Ali would wheel me down an alley behind the mud-walled stalls of the bazaar. It was soggy and brown and an open sewer ran the length of it. Out of view, I could stretch. We didn't earn much, but now, when it snowed, we had enough for a few days' stay in a teahouse. This is how we survived our third winter.

One day as we returned to the bazaar, a grocer named Rafi Jan confronted us. He had a thick black beard and a round hard stomach. Long ago we'd learned to avoid his stall. Under his arm, he carried a large sack of rice. He looked down his pointed nose at us and shouted: Here's your zakat, boy!

He dropped the sack on me. Its weight knocked over the wheelbarrow. My legs shot straight out before I landed in a heap on the dirt floor. Merchants stepped from behind their stalls and shoppers gathered around me.

This boy is no cripple! announced Rafi Jan to the crowd.

A wave of laughter rose up through the bazaar. Shame made my stomach crumple like paper. I fought my desire to cry. Even a boy can lose his nang.

I pulled myself up from the dust of the road and as I did, Ali ran past. Rafi Jan continued to laugh, blinded by his own fat hilarity, the huge mass of his stomach lifting. Ali threw his fist into Rafi Jan's groin. The merchant's laughter choked and he fell onto his side, the dust settling onto the perfect blackness of his beard.

Hanzeer! Ali screamed over him. Next time I'll kill you!

A silence fell over the bazaar. Then, one by one, the merchants laughed harder than before. While Rafi Jan lay there, his nang in the dirt, another merchant approached us. He wore plain clothes, a serious face, and carried a heap of twisted branches in his arms. He introduced himself as Hamza.

You understand how to defend your brother's nang, he said to Ali. You know something of Pashtunwali. That is all too rare in these days. I could use a young man like you. Untangle these branches and deliver them as kindling to the Rish Khor Teahouse. You know the one?

Ali nodded. We'd stayed there once. It was far away, on the north side of the city.

Good, said Hamza. This will be yours when you return.

He held up a 500-Afghani note, enough for a day's food.

We sorted the wood into piles and lashed bundles of each. It took us nearly an hour to get to the teahouse and the same to return. By this time, the stalls of the bazaar were closed, but Hamza was still there, rocking back on two legs of a worn wooden stool. When he saw us, he reached into the shirt pocket of his baggy shalwar kameez. Pinched between his fingers was the 500-Afghani note. Ali snatched it from Hamza. Holding the note, my brother put his eyes to the ground, ashamed by his desperation.

I need someone to watch my shop tonight, said Hamza. If you boys do that, others will likely have business for you in the morning.

You would trust us with your shop? asked Ali.

I ask no man to trust me and I trust no one. Trust is a burden one puts on another. Then he spoke the proverb: *But he is my friend that grinds at my mill.*

Hamza left us two blankets and an oil lamp. We wrapped ourselves in them and placed the lamp between us. Our blankets smelled of straw and dirt, the lamp of diesel. It was warm inside the stall, and we slept.

In the morning there was work. The other merchants agreed – it was difficult to find someone who'd make an honest delivery for a 500-Afghani note. All through that winter and the following seasons, Ali and I hauled goods to and from the bazaar. Flour to the bakers, bolts of fabric to the tailors, we stacked our wheelbarrow's load so its height often exceeded our own. We'd soon earned enough money to buy a handcart or even a mule, but Ali refused to spend it. Instead he saved every coin, and at the end of each day the last merchant to close up would let us sleep on the dirt floor of his shop.

The next fall was our fourth away from home. This is when the Americans came. The militants in Orgun hid in the border mountains. At night they'd return. Some were Haqqanis, I think, but most now called themselves Taliban. A few were honourable men who practised Pashtunwali, but many did as they pleased, taking what they wanted from homes and shops. We heard stories of far greater crimes outside Orgun. Militants accused men of being informants and beheaded them in front of their families. Americans accused men of being militants and disappeared them in the night on helicopters. The militants fought to protect us from the Americans and the Americans fought to protect us from the militants, and being so protected, life was very dangerous. Those who came to the market from smaller, far-off villages spoke of gun battles and bombings. We learned the names of commanders such as Sabir, Hafez, and later, Gazan. They fought on all sides and lived with us like shadows, like those of the boys we'd once slept beside in the mountains. The merchants in the bazaar picked no side. The politics of their war never changed – survival. Ali and I continued to make deliveries. We also gave the merchants a watchful set of eyes at night. For this we were valued and that seemed very good.

One night more than a year after Ali punched Rafi Jan, now one of our best customers, my brother said he had a gift for me. I asked him what it was, but he would tell me nothing. Instead, he turned down the flame of the oil lamp that sat between us on the floor. The room grew dark and he held his index finger to the sky as he spoke.

Look there, Aziz, what do you see?

Father's ring, I said. The ring shone in the dim lamplight, and I thought perhaps he would give it to me.

Khar, donkey! Ali snapped, and clapped me on the back of the head. I point at the moon and you stare at my finger. Do you see the moon, there?

I looked past his finger and through a small shuttered window.

Yes, I said. I see it.

And what do you know of it?

It is a half-moon tonight.

Do you know why? Ali asked.

No.

No, he repeated. Do you feel any shame that you don't know?

You don't know either, I reminded him.

You're right, he said. I don't. But I feel shame because of it.

Between us it became quiet.

And this, Father's ring, he said. How would you replace it if it were lost?

I would never lose it.

Someday it will be lost, he said. And if we haven't learned to replace it, the loss will be complete.

If you give it to me, I said, it will never be lost.

I very much wanted the ring.

Ali shook his head and spoke: That is what those fools in the mountains say, give it all to me and it will never be lost. They create nothing and so the little over which they fight is already lost. You will learn another way. I have been saving our money so you might start at the madrassa.

Who will help you with work? I asked, hurt by Ali's wish to be without me.

That is my burden now, he said. Your burden is to be educated. It's what Father wanted for me. It's what I can give you. To make something new.

I won't abandon you, I said.

To not go, you abandon me.

These last words he spoke the strongest of all.

*

For a long time that is how it was. I went to the madrassa each day and in the evening I returned to the bazaar. Ali never let me help with the deliveries. He insisted I study. I sat against one of the bazaar's stalls, reciting the Holy Qur'an or my math, the two subjects we learned. At night we stayed in whatever shop hosted us. We lay on the floor, on opposite sides of our oil lamp, staring at it. The jerking flame became all that moved between us.

Tell me what you're learning, Ali whispered.

Ask me how many aayaaths there are, I said.

He asked and quickly I gave the answer.

There are 6,666 aayaaths in the Holy Qur'an. Ask me my multiplication tables.

He asked what 13 times 13 was, but my math didn't always come as quickly. Soon I figured the way of it and answered, 169, and Ali listened carefully as I went on, telling him how we'd soon be taught algebra and the other holy texts such as the Bukhari. He asked me what algebra was, but I didn't know how to explain it. The imam had only told us that we would learn it, not what it was. And in this way, Ali would listen to me until he fell asleep.

Always he fell asleep first, and always I turned off the lamp between us.

★

Whatever small life we'd built unravelled on a grey afternoon in winter. The air was hard and cold. It was the day of Ashura, almost five years since the Americans came. I left the madrassa and was walking back to the bazaar. The fast had not yet broken, but already people piled into the streets. Sombre marches carried the crowds towards the mosque where in the night they'd commemorate the ancient martyrs.

I walked through the alleys, jumping over the open sewers, avoiding the crowd. Suddenly a shaking like thunder overcame the city with a noise like steel down a washboard. I stopped. Alone in the alley, I searched the rooftops. Dark smoke curled upward from the bazaar. My body stiffened with fear. I stepped into the crowd. They rushed towards the smoke and the violence which just occurred. I didn't follow them. I ran to the hospital instead. If there were something to learn of my brother, I would not find out as a victim in the street.

I arrived at the hospital red-faced and gasping. I shouldered through the swinging double doors. Inside the echoes of my breath travelled the long linoleum hallway. Apart from this, it was quiet. A doctor with a young face and neat-trimmed moustache grabbed my wrist.

No one has arrived yet, he said. When they do come, make yourself useful. Help unload the ambulances.

I stood in the dim corridor with the hospital staff. Sirens wailed in the distance. Everyone pulled on rubber gloves. Nurses rolled out gurneys made up with white sheets. The sirens' noise rose and fell, closer and closer, and my stomach followed the rhythm, sick with sound. Hold this, said an old sinewy nurse. He placed my hand on a gurney. The task steadied me.

The wounded and dead arrived together. Two paramedics threw open the hospital's double doors, backing their ambulance into the main corridor. Its well-dented fender crashed into either side of the jamb. Its decrepit engine sputtered exhaust in our faces.

Unload them outside! shouted one of the doctors.

The paramedics ignored the doctor and began to empty the ambulance. Inside bodies were stacked on each other. We pulled them apart just as my brother once pulled apart the twisted branches he bundled and delivered as kindling from the bazaar.

Take what you can in the gurneys! shouted a paramedic. Carry the rest!

Hurry, there are more still in the bazaar! shouted another.

We unloaded bodies onto the gurneys. Soon we pulled off the sheets. It was easier to clean the slickness from the plain rubber mattresses. When we ran out of gurneys we heaved bodies onto our shoulders and carried them to the operating room. The ambulance sped away. The old nurse grasped my arm again. His sad eyes fell towards the ground and rested on a large man whose clothes had been burned from him. He rolled the man to his back. It was Rafi Jan. The only part of him I recognised was the fatness I once despised and his singed beard. He was too far gone to notice me. Either the old nurse didn't see the shock on my face or didn't care. He lifted Rafi Jan onto my shoulders. Against my neck Rafi Jan's burned skin felt like the curled bark of a tree. I expected him to scream but he was silent. He wasn't yet dead, but he'd already crossed over. I'd once wished badal against this fat man who'd laughed at me. Knowing this, I felt both guilt and, it shames me to say, satisfaction.

Some of the wounded cried out, most did not. Many looked at their broken bodies with curiosity, as if in a new suffering existed a chance to escape the old one. The last ambulance returned with only two men. I recognised neither. We brought them inside. Outside the hospital fell quiet.

My brother arrived in the back of a cheap binjo. His waist was wet and red. A sheet covered an emptiness where his left leg would have been. He grasped a slick trash bag, his knuckles white with effort. In it was the leg. His cheeks looked like green ash and his eyes swam about his face. Tears poured over his temples.

He saw me and propped himself up on his elbows. His body failed him and he lay back down. He stared at nothing, looking past, but not at me. We loaded him onto a gurney. I moved to whisper in his ear, but found myself with nothing to say. I hung my head close to his.

Zakat for my poor brother the cripple, he whispered. Zakat, zakat, zakat . . .

No, no, I assured him. There are many who walk again.

His eyes rolled. He breathed, panting.

There is more gone, he said.

The old nurse pushed the gurney inside. I ran next to it.

Let me tell you what I learned today, I said. The imam explained algebra.

I put my hand on Ali's head. The sweat in his hair was cool and slick. He looked away, saying nothing. I continued: It comes from the ancient Arabs. In their language it means to make whole from parts.

It is enough, Ali said.

He shut his eyes. The moustached doctor, the one with the young face, stood outside the operating room. He held up his arm. No further, he said. They rolled Ali past. I sat in the hallway against the wall. I could hear only the squeak of a loose metal axle. The old nurse wheeled a steel mop and bucket down the far end of the corridor. Dark red blood pools stained the linoleum. The mop slopped down. Water leaked from its braids. The old nurse swayed back and forth, spreading the dark red into light. I brought my knees to my chest and rested my head between my arms.

I fell asleep.

*

Hours later, I woke up in the hallway. It was morning. I searched for my brother. The room where he'd been wheeled was now full of empty beds and shining trays of surgical equipment. The night before felt like a tear in my memory. I left the room and wandered the corridors. I didn't recognise any of the doctors or nurses. At the far end of the main corridor, away from the double doors, was a steel desk. Behind it, hunched over his work, sat a small man with sharp shoulders and a cratered face. His oily hair was neatly parted. It gleamed even in the dimness. I placed my palms on his desk.

My brother was brought here last night, I said. I can't find him.

His name and injury? asked the man.

Ali Iqtbal, I said. He lost his leg.

My throat choked against the words. From a drawer in his desk, the man pulled out a folder filled with handwritten lists. He sorted through the reams of lined paper, scrawled with blue ink. He slid the mess back in the folder, shook his head, and tossed the stack into the drawer.

These are all the ones with missing legs, he said. Your brother is not here.

He is here. He was brought in last night and wheeled into there, I said, pointing to the surgery ward. Look again, Ali Iqtbal.

He may be here, answered the man, but he's not on my list. They've been adding names all morning. Check back later.

He palmed down a few licks of fallen hair.

I stepped from the desk and looked along the hallway. At its far end stood two men. From their mouths, I could see words passing quietly and quickly between them. One of the men was light-skinned, clearly an American. He'd grown a large beard, but its bush was an unconvincing disguise, thick and blond as it was. I could feel his eyes rest on me from behind the sunglasses he wore even inside. He spoke a last word to the other man and walked away. This other man walked towards me, talking loudly.

What's the problem, brother?

He spoke perfect Pashto, but wore an American uniform. He took a few steps closer. I wanted no dealings with an American, but when I got a better look at him and saw his hooked nose, high cheekbones, and lean muscled frame, I knew he was a Pashto.

My brother, I can't find him, I said.

He came in last night? asked the man, his question reeking of cigarettes.

I nodded.

After Gazan's attack? he added.

I'm not sure. It was after the attack at the bazaar.

Yes, Gazan's attack, said the man. As for your brother, you are not asking the right people. Come.

He led me up a flight of stairs to the second floor. We walked down another linoleum hallway and arrived at a corner door. A stencil on the door read HOSPITAL SUPERVISOR.

What is your name? he asked me.

Aziz Iqtbal. My brother is Ali.

Very good, I am Taqbir, said the man. I'll take care of this for you.

I crouched against the wall and waited. As I did, I saw two other men dressed like Taqbir walking up and down the corridor. They wore the same green-and-brown-spotted uniform. Every so often, they entered one of the private rooms or spoke with family members who waited outside. They'd kneel, place a wife or grandmother's hand between theirs, speaking quietly. Though the two seemed gentle and earnest, I felt suspicious of them.

After a few minutes, Taqbir returned. I have found Ali, he said. But there is something you should know.

I looked back at him, stupid and afraid.

Taqbir continued: His name is not listed with those who lost a limb.

But I saw him. His leg was missing.

That may be so, he answered. But Ali is listed as having a serious injury to the organs.

He paused.

I stared back. Taqbir watched me, hoping I understood.

As a man, he said, your brother is no longer complete.

Tightness spread across my chest, through my throat, and into my mouth and eyes. It spread as a web does, weaving into parts what was once whole. Taqbir rested his hand along my shoulder. He fixed a solid stare at me. I wanted his strength.

It is only right that you should know this now, he said. You will need to be strong when you see him.

I nodded.

It had not occurred to me that I would need to be strong for Ali. I'd hoped some assurance of his might allow me to accept what happened. But this horror was for all time. To survive, Ali now relied on me.

I thanked Taqbir, but I didn't want to thank anyone, my resentment was so great for all I'd lost. I felt very small standing next to him. I looked into the grey flecks of his eyes, like a hawk's, and at his face, with its sharp and certain angles. All of it offered me nothing but pity.

We walked outside, to a yard behind the hospital's main building. Here the ground was hardpan dirt. On it rose a large three-pole military tent. Parked next to the tent were two ambulances. A few of the paramedics I'd seen last night stood around them, their stares full of sympathy. They understood my situation. I tensed my face into a blank mask.

Taqbir parted the green canvas flap with his arm and warm fumes of sweat, smoke, and blood pulled us inside. In the tent's centre two stoves burned and the sap of the wood crackled and spit. The chimneys consisted of hollowed cooking-oilcans stacked and nailed together. They leaked. Cots lined the tent so closely that there was no room between them. Doctors climbed onto the ends of the cots, hovering above their patients.

I walked the rows, searching for my brother. Many of the men had bandaged faces. I looked for a missing leg. I could only identify Ali by his loss. And soon I saw it. A white sheet rested flatly where something was gone. Gauze covered the hollow of Ali's left eye. At his waist, a sopping red wound was dressed with an adult diaper.

His head rested away from me. From beneath his gown and bedsheet, his knee and shoulders poked up like the three poles of the tent. My tears came silently. I had nothing to say to my brother, no strength to offer him. To be crippled as he was takes all of a man. It takes his nang.

An orderly passed by. I grabbed his arm. He looked back at me with flat eyes that showed nothing. Why is my brother here instead of in the hospital? I asked.

This is the outpatient ward, he said.

From my mouth words came in a shout, surprising me: These men are not ready to be discharged!

Not all patients get well, he said. We will keep him here for a couple of days. A longer stay can only be arranged through the hospital supervisor.

Taqbir watched me from the tent's flap. He picked the dirt from his fingernails with a long commando knife he'd pulled from his belt. I rushed towards him, pleading: Unless something is arranged my brother cannot stay here.

Taqbir kissed his teeth and patted my shoulder. I'll check, he said, wait here.

He walked past me and down the rows of cots towards Ali. I stood by the tent flap. Taqbir leaned over my brother. He kissed his teeth again and shook his head. At the foot of Ali's cot was a stool. On it sat his cell phone, prayer beads, and my father's ring. Taqbir picked up the ring, but left the rest. He whistled and waved his hand to the expressionless orderly. I couldn't hear the words spoken between them, but the orderly knowingly pointed at each of my brother's wounds. Taqbir listened and continued to shake his head solemnly.

Taking his time, Taqbir walked back up the rows of cots, inspecting the broken bodies on either side of him as a commander reviews his troops. Every few steps he stopped and looked down his nose, considering one of the heaps that lined the tent. His inspection complete, Taqbir planted himself at my shoulder. Come, he said, we must see if something can be arranged. Ali is in a dangerous condition. As we turned to leave, Taqbir placed the ring in my palm.

You should care for this until your brother is better.

I'd lacked even the courage to speak to my brother, but now I slid his ring, the ring of my father, on my finger.

Taqbir smiled at me. Good, he said. And I noticed his many gold teeth.

*

From his black leather chair, the hospital supervisor waved us into his office. He turned off the flat-screen Hitachi that hung from a ceiling mount by the door and removed his feet from his wood-panelled desk. On its top was an empty in-box. He tossed the remote control into it. Carved across the front of the desk, in an elaborate script, was an aayaath I'd learned in the madrassa: *There comes forth from their bellies a drink of diverse hues wherein is healing for all mankind.*

Two brown leather sofas, stained with watermarks, sat on either side of a glass table. Spread across the table were steel dishes, the rims pressed with a floral print, each one filled with pine nuts, raisins, and pistachios. The office was arranged to impress, but it did not seem like a place where work was done.

Come in, come in, said the supervisor to Taqbir. Who is your young friend?

The supervisor was a small fat man. On his bald head, the ceiling lights shined in a crown. His neck and cheeks hung towards the ground, heavy with age and fat. He took out a cheap paper packet of Seven Stars. Before he could open them, Taqbir tossed him a pack of Marlboro Reds. The supervisor smiled, pulled back the cardboard top, and sniffed them. He smiled again and extended the cigarettes towards us. Taqbir held up his palm. The supervisor lit one and greedily inhaled. As the rich American tobacco filled his lungs, he hacked into the bend of his elbow. While he did, Taqbir spoke: This is Aziz. His brother was very badly wounded in yesterday's bombing.

The supervisor shook his head and slowly regained his breath. Gazan is a dog to do these things, he said. He's become bold. A bombing in the bazaar! And what will the Americans do? They give so little to those who support them. Perhaps after this bombing they will be more generous, but enough of this. Please, you must be hungry.

He gestured towards the plates on the glass table. I hadn't eaten since the day before. I filled one hand with raisins and the other with pine nuts.

How can I help you? asked the supervisor.

My brother is in the outpatient ward after only one night, but his wounds are still serious.

This is a hard thing, he answered. These days a hospital is less a place for healing than for dying.

The supervisor moved to the opposite sofa. He leaned forwards, picking at a few pistachios. As he ate white spittle formed on the corners of his lips. He looked around the room with an empty stare as though he were solving an equation – my brother's life, my livelihood, and his hospital's vacancies divided one into the other. Turning towards his desk, he continued: It is as the Aayaath says, *healing for all mankind*. I must weigh each man against another. My position is very difficult.

Surely something can be done, said Taqbir.

There is only so much I can do, said the supervisor. My heart wants to help this boy, but we must be practical.

He turned his eyes towards the ceiling.

If there were more, said Taqbir, could his brother be kept here?

The supervisor stood from the sofa. With a fresh handful of pistachios, he circled the room. Of course, he said, but more of what? Where is there more of anything these days?

More money, said Taqbir.

If I had such money, I would pay the fees myself, said the supervisor. Do not misunderstand me. My every desire is to help.

And if I paid the fees? asked Taqbir.

I can't repay you, I interrupted, but Taqbir's outstretched hand silenced me.

The supervisor stroked his fat face, and said: If expenses are covered there will be no problem.

Then the matter is settled, replied Taqbir.

He stood, bowed, and motioned for the two of us to leave. The supervisor sat back in his chair and put his feet on the desk. He reached forwards, took the remote from his in-box, and turned on the Hitachi. As I walked out the door, he called behind me: Taqbir is a man of great generosity. You are blessed to call him a friend.

I never saw the hospital supervisor again.

*

We left the office and stood in the corridor. Taqbir took a fresh pack of Marlboro Reds from his pocket. He lit one and looked at me. He frowned with disappointment.

You are not happy that your brother is saved? he asked.

I am.

He took another pull on his cigarette. You know from my uniform that I am a military man, he said, but do you know about the Special Lashkar?

I shook my head.

We work in the south of the province, he added. Near a town called Shkin. You know of Shkin, yes?

I nodded, but had never been. Shkin was a day's drive south. As I would learn, to call it a town was generous. It was really fifteen mud huts along the high desert plain of the Pakistani border. To the south of it, the plain rose into wild mountains, remote villages, and a savage, isolated war.

We fight against the Taliban to uphold Pashtunwali, said Taqbir. The Special Lashkar protects the border and keeps men like Gazan in their place.

So you fight for the government?

We fight for the nang of our homes, but for no government, answered Taqbir. He stuck his chest out in his clean American uniform.

So I am to serve in the Special Lashkar?

You are lucky for a chance to strike back at Gazan, answered Taqbir. In badal there is nang for you, and for what has been taken from your brother. As long as you fight, Ali will be cared for here.

I had no one but Ali. To care for him was my single alternative. And single alternatives have a logic all their own. Men go to war with such a logic, and my thinking was that of a young man, clear and unclouded by experience and doubt.

When do I leave? I replied.

Taqbir reached into his cargo pocket. He handed me a slip of paper no bigger than a matchbook. You know of the American base near here, the one outside Sharana village? he said.

I nodded. The helicopters from FOB Sharana often flew over Orgun. Following their flight patterns, the FOB was a day's walk north, or so I'd heard.

Go to its back gate tomorrow, he said. Call this number. Tell them your name and that you are going to Shkin.

You aren't coming with me? I asked.

Bring only what you must, he said, seeming not to hear me. Everything will be provided.

Then I will meet you in Shkin, I said.

What makes you think I work at that firebase? Taqbir spoke his words coldly.

I thought you were a soldier, I replied.

I am, he said, but not a common one as you will be. My work is here, and you should thank me for it. There are others who would welcome such generosity.

I stared at Taqbir. In his hard face and crisp uniform I could see a part of my future, but I understood none of it. I was now a servant, maybe not to Taqbir, but to men like him.

I answered: I'll be there and am grateful.

He nodded, still taking his measure of me.

We shook hands and Taqbir wished me luck and long life. I walked towards the hospital's main double doors. As I put my shoulder into one, I looked back. Standing at the far end of the corridor, I saw Taqbir join the American with the blond beard. Together they spoke quietly. Then the two strolled off in search of another recruit.

THAT NIGHT, I slept in the hills among the orphaned boys. I lacked the courage to visit Ali for a last time, and in the morning I departed. I walked without rest, guided by the helicopters that passed steadily above. When the sun set, I could see FOB Sharana spread low across the dust of the plain and the small airfield on it. A ditch ran around the FOB. The dirt from it filled the HESCO barriers of the perimeter wall. These were stacked three high with coils of concertina wire running on top. Their steel frames and burlap linings had splits and tears. This made the wall sag. In places the earth in the HESCOs spilled back into the ditch from where it was dug. In the back of the FOB, I found the HESCOs laid out in a serpentine. These led to a tall steel gate. A light from a tower shined onto the ground in front of the gate. Under the spotlight, the ground was bright as day. Next to it stood an Afghan guard in a plywood booth. He noticed me just before I stepped onto the ground where the light shone. He stepped into his booth and grabbed a radio.

I froze.

Slowly I took out my phone and called Taqbir's contact. A voice answered: How did you get this number?

I am Aziz, I said, a friend of Taqbir's. I am at the entrance.

Hold on, said the voice. It sounded as if the phone had been set down. I stood and watched the guard. Then the voice returned: Yes, Aziz, I will call you back.

The phone disconnected.

I waited. The gate guard continued to watch me from across the serpentine. He began to talk into his radio. I wanted to leave. Then my phone rang.

Tell the guard that you are on Flight 873 to Shkin, said the voice.

That is all? I asked.

Still the guard stared at me. It was as if we were having a silent conversation, one with the other, me speaking into my phone and he into his radio.

That is all, said the voice, hanging up.

I approached. The guard put down his radio and stepped from his booth, rubbing his eyes sleepily. His khaki uniform was too small and his brown suede boots too large. The thick mat of stubble on his cheeks was unkempt and seemed the result of laziness, not any effort to grow a beard.

I gave him my flight number. Shkin, eh? he said, grinning. You don't look like a soldier.

How does a soldier look? I asked.

Not like you.

He banged against the gate with the butt of his Kalashnikov. Another guard ran down from his tower to open it. We stood, waiting. Shkin's a brutal place, he told me.

It is, I said, my words not quite a statement but not a question either.

Good hunting for a soldier, he said, but I think it is better to be on the gate.

Maybe, I replied.

He laughed at me. You see, he said, you are no soldier.

How do you know that?

Soldiers don't want to watch gates.

Soon I'll be a soldier, I said, finding confidence.

Maybe you will be, but I'll never know. The flights to Shkin carry soldiers, but the flights back never do. He shook his head in an unkind way.

A door was cut and hinged into the gate so it didn't have to be opened fully each time. The other guard poked his head through it.

Him? he asked.

Yes, to Shkin, said the guard.

Now they both shook their heads.

Good hunting, said the gate guard as I entered the FOB. I couldn't tell if he were wishing me luck or making another statement about the fighting. I was glad to leave him.

Inside, metal stakes threaded with rope formed a pen in the dust. This was the holding area for the helicopter flights. Afghan soldiers filled it. They wore a mix of green, khaki, and blue uniforms. None wore the camouflage pattern I'd seen on Taqbir. I had no uniform and they eyed me with suspicion.

Evening turned to night. Tucking my legs to my chest, I dozed on the cold dirt. Each hour a thin, clean-shaven Afghan, and an American with enormous muscles and cheeks red as bee stings walked into the holding area. The Afghan read names and destinations from a list while the American supervised. The crowd thinned out around me. Soon a chubby Afghan in shalwar kameez was the only other who remained. He seemed to be no soldier at all and he sat atop white bags of rice that rested on a pallet. Each of the bags was solid as a large mud brick. On their fronts, printed neatly in red and blue, were the letters *USAID*.

The Afghan and the American returned. Even though there were just two of us left, the Afghan called our names and destinations from his list. Aziz Iqtbal, Shkin! I stood and patted the dust from my clothes. Naseeb Ilyas, Shkin! The chubby man slid off his pallet.

The Afghan waved a forklift towards Naseeb's rice. Its hydraulic controls whined as the steel prongs came up then down, aligning to the open ends of the pallet. The prongs paused for a moment and then stabbed under the pallet, heaving it to such a height that in order to steer, the driver leaned out the side of the cab. The load bounced as it moved across the uneven ground, before settling along the cement taxiway of the airfield. Naseeb and I walked behind. The night around us was so dark that I couldn't see the rows of helicopters and jet planes I knew lined our path. I only felt the smooth concrete under my feet and also disappointment. I'd never seen a jet plane up close and now probably never would. We walked quickly and the fat man, Naseeb, panted behind me.

Are you a new soldier? he asked.

I considered the roundness of his face. His skin looked like the uneven moon cheese that shone down at us. I am a friend of Taqbir's, I said. He offered me a soldier's job.

Yes, yes, the place you're going is full of Taqbir's friends, said Naseeb. Every time we lose one, he sends us another.

You work in Shkin? I asked.

He pointed towards his pallet. I am the supply officer, he said. A thankless job but one that enjoys Commander Sabir's complete trust. To fight in a unit led by him is a great honour.

I said nothing, unsure how to show the proper respect to Commander Sabir, a man I'd yet to know.

There are more recruits like you in Shkin, said Naseeb.

One by one they've arrived this winter, training until the warm weather comes and the fighting season begins. There were eight when I left a week ago, maybe more now.

I am ready, I said.

He was quiet for a moment. When he spoke again, there was more weight in his voice: No doubt you heard of Gazan's bombing in the bazaar.

I shrugged. There was nothing I wanted to say to him about that.

In the villages south of here it is even worse, he said. Those dogs attack and then hide in the mountains. What nang can be claimed in that?

I shook my head.

Yes, yes, he added, nodding to himself. The hunting will be good this fighting season. There are more Americans here and Gazan is tired and we will—

Distant thumps and a low shrieking squeezed out all other noise. We saw nothing and still the noise came. A hot wind surged downward. It spilled like a pitcher of water across the ground, pasting our baggy clothes to our bodies. The helicopter settled in front of us. The other sounds returned and the gust became a warm breeze in the cold night. The back ramp lowered, opening like a fist. Inside, blue overhead lights shined dimly into a long empty hull that shook, as if with a sickness, under the motors above. A pair of crew members ran up and down, unlashing bundles from the deck plates, clearing the cargo hold. Their night-vision goggles covered the tops of their faces except where two coins of green demon light shone onto their eyes. They wore dark one-piece jumpsuits, olive-green, maybe black. Each of their helmets was painted like a giant skull, white on black. A protective face mask formed the jawbone, decorated

33

with jagged teeth. The two helmets were identical except that one of the crew members had decorated his with a red Mohawk that ran its length.

The crew waved us on board. I followed Naseeb to a canvas bench near the front. Naseeb slid his shoulders beneath a set of straps. He pulled another set across his lap and fastened three buckles into a fourth with a circular clasp. I watched. Then I imitated him and slid my buckles into the clasp, but I was much smaller than whoever had sat in my seat before. Soon my loose straps were tangled. I tried to tighten them but couldn't. I attempted to fit the loose straps into the clasp as Naseeb had done, but the buckles would not lock. As I struggled, Naseeb took pity on me. He loosened his own straps, leaned across his seat, tightened mine, and then pressed a button I hadn't seen on the clasp's front. He sat back down, tightened his straps, and nodded at me. Now that we were both seated, the forklift driver lowered his night-vision goggles and drove the pallet of rice in behind us. The crew lashed it to the floor. The ramp closed, the helicopter rattled. In an instant we became smooth and weightless. I smiled in the dark. I'd never flown before.

*

Less than an hour later, the helicopter lifted back and its engines screamed and rattled, easing us downward. I looked out the window but saw nothing. We landed with a heavy bounce. The blue lights came on again. The ramp lowered and the crew rolled the pallet into the gravel-and-dirt landing zone. Naseeb and I followed. Outside we hugged our bodies against the bags of rice as the helicopter's engines pushed hot air against us. Its dead weight lifted and then disappeared.

My ears rang in the silence and my eyes strained in the dark. There was no one there. Naseeb walked off the landing zone.

I grabbed his arm. Where do I sleep? I asked.

You see that light? he answered. Away from us blinked a dim slit. That is the barracks for the recruits, he said. Then Naseeb turned from me and walked into the night, leaving his pallet on the landing zone.

A heavy felt blanket was tacked over a HESCO doorway. It blew in the breeze. The light behind it escaped, in and out, in and out. Mud and rock swelled the steel frames of the HESCOs, buckling them slowly. Inside, a stove full of embers held out against the cold. A thin dusty carpet struggled to cover the dirt floor. Under short wool blankets eight lumps slept with their knees huddled to their chests. I lay in the corner and crawled into myself for warmth. I had no blanket and was the ninth.

*

I woke an hour before sunrise, worrying about my brother and if Taqbir had kept his promise to me. As long as I worried, my sleep had no depth, so I left the barracks and looked for a warm place until dawn. Somewhere outside a generator hummed. I walked quickly through the firebase, towards the sound and the hope of warmth. I found the generator next to a trailer full of latrines. I stepped inside. It was clean and simple. A large mirror, two sinks, and two rows of toilets – not your Western kind, but stalls built around holes in the ground. I squatted down to use one and, still worrying about my brother, I dozed.

Suddenly I heard the noise of a truck outside and then footsteps as someone entered. Water ran from one of the faucets. I strained to see between the stall's cracks, and noticed the very blond beard from the hospital. The man pulled clothes from a bag – a few T-shirts and some underwear and blue jeans. No uniforms, just regular clothes. He washed them in the sink with a bar of hand soap. As he did, he whistled to himself some happy tune. He didn't catch my feet under the stall. I dared not move.

The door slammed again. There was another set of steps. I angled my head and caught the first glimpse of a man I would come to know well, Issaq. He had a dwarfish look common to those for whom starvation was a childhood companion. His strange appearance made me question whether I was in fact awake, or he real. He stood at the sink next to the blond man and ran a rag under the water. He took off his shirt and scrubbed with the rag under his arms and against his shoulders. I only caught glimpses, but what I saw frightened me. Scars crossed his body in every direction. The skin around each was cracked and dry. Issaq itched at the tangle of scars with his wet rag. Soon they became red and looked evil, like sleeping snakes beneath his skin.

The blond man stood next to Issaq, wringing water from his shirts and underpants. For a time neither spoke, but in that quiet lay a familiarity. Item by item, the blond man hung his clothes on the edge of an empty sink. Stencilled on a waistband or shirt collar, I saw his name – JACK.

Finally, Mr Jack broke the silence. How are the recruits? he asked. His Pashto was like a child's. He invented unusual pronunciations for common words.

They are fine, said Issaq, but I wonder how long they will stay.

Are they scared to fight? asked Mr Jack.

Issaq turned towards him, displaying his body's many scars. That has never been a problem for us, he said. He stood there for a moment longer, forcing Mr Jack to look at him. Satisfied,

Issaq faced back to the mirror. He spoke into his reflection: It has been two months since we've been paid.

I've seen Sabir tonight, said Mr Jack. He has plenty for everyone now.

Issaq was quiet for a moment. Would you like to come to training tomorrow, to see the recruits? he asked.

Mr Jack answered: I would, but my trip was only for tonight, to see Sabir.

When you're next here, they will be ready, said Issaq, proudly.

Train them hard, Mr Jack said. The spring will be busy.

We are always busy, Issaq grumbled.

I don't think Mr Jack understood him, though. He'd spoken quickly and, as I've said, Mr Jack's Pashto was not so good. I leaned back and stopped looking at the two of them. I heard the faucet turn off. There were more steps. Outside a truck door slammed shut. The engine's noise fell into the distance and Mr Jack was gone.

I was very still. I strained to hear. Steps came towards me. A set of boots planted themselves in front of my stall.

Issaq kicked the door open, just missing my head.

You flush! You wipe! Then you flush! Yes?

My bare ass still squatted above the hole. I couldn't shift my gaze from his scarred chest. Above it, his green eyes stared wildly at me. His face was like a worn-in hide pulled tight over high cheekbones. His pants were the same American uniform I'd seen on Taqbir, but the burning red henna painted onto his fingernails and dyed into his hair, in the traditional way, made it impossible for him to be mistaken for anything but the Pashto warrior he was.

I said nothing, followed his instructions, and rushed back to the recruit barracks, where I would be cold but safe.

A little while later, just before the sun rose, Issaq pulled the blanket from our door. In the dim light, he lifted four sandbags inside. I crouched in the far corner. He knifed open the top of each. A splash of dirt flew across the room as he tossed the contents on us. All the while he shouted: Up! Up! Spey zoy! Sons of swine! Get out of your own filth! Clenched in his teeth was a whistle. He blew it with all the muscles of his stomach. The other recruits jumped from their blankets. I stood frozen in the back corner, using the great defence of the powerless – anonymity.

We dressed quickly. I stole glances at the other recruits, wondering what type of men they were. In truth, they were barely men. Like me, most were not past twenty. I felt a kinship, but also a distrust of them. A misfortune, like mine, had surely brought them here, but I remembered those first two winters in Orgun and what Ali had taught me about the boys we'd slept among in the hills. Just like before, I would be a fool to trust someone as poor as me.

We jammed through the door and into a small, dusty court-yard. The firebase was little more than ten plywood huts sur-rounded by HESCO barriers. The dawn fell in shadow along the mountains and Issaq chased circles around us, his energy rising with the sun. Issaq's voice awoke the feral dogs that slept between the huts. They stretched their limbs in the cold morn-ing air, offering us curious looks. A tall and skinny recruit with sandy hair ran outside in bare feet. He clutched a pair of sandals to his chest. When he bent over to put them on, his trousers slid down his waist. This was Tawas. Issaq! he shouted, calling our tormentor by his first name only. I soon learned there was no rank in the Special Lashkar. Everyone's position was known by an unspoken authority, the idea being that anyone who relied on rank to lead was unfit for the role.

Issaq rushed over to Tawas and thrust his chest at him, his ribs pressing into what must have been, at best, Tawas's stomach. What? Issaq said, spitting out the words.

Tawas stood at attention. With one hand he grasped his waistband. I've forgotten my belt, he mumbled.

Issaq reached up and struck him with an open palm across the face. Go back and get it! he shouted.

Short commanders are the most difficult. They carry disappointment too openly. If they turn their disappointment on themselves they become timid. If they turn it on others they become tyrants.

Issaq was a tyrant.

Through the rest of winter, he taught us the foundation of all soldiering – repetition. That first day was like every other. After we awoke, we ran to the empty helicopter-landing zone. Soaked and gasping for air, we crawled through the wet mud and gravel while Issaq stood over us. We did push-ups and sit-ups on the loose rocks that scraped our palms and cut our backs. We wore only our thin shalwar kameez, uniforms being a privilege we'd yet to earn. Between exercises Issaq paused and pondered how to increase our agonies. He lacked imagination, so we often did more of the same. Had he been creative he could've designed no better torture than the sameness of this routine.

Always Issaq taunted us. He'd hold his head back, asking the sky, or perhaps God, how we'd be ready to fight Gazan's men in the spring. How will I convince a fierce commander like Sabir that these darwankee are soldiers, he'd mutter to himself, spitting in the dirt, as if in the cold muck he'd found our faces. When Issaq got bored, he made us run laps inside the HESCO walls of the perimeter. The feral dogs trotted alongside us, as if in solidarity.

Once Issaq tired of this, he lined us up in formation. We stood covered in mud as he brought over his beloved motorbike, a small red thing with tan stuffing that bulged from its duct-taped seat. Tawas later told me the bike had been confiscated on a raid two summers past. A man had tried to escape on it. He'd driven right in front of Issaq, and Issaq had shot him in the face with his pistol. Issaq insisted this made the bike his. After the raid, and against Commander Sabir's wishes, he'd driven it eight hours back to the firebase.

From the formation's front Issaq shouted: Right turn, march! Forwards, march! Double quick, march! His motorcycle putt-ered into gear. We ran after him, out the candy-striped gate and down the dusty hilltop that wore our firebase like a crown. We set out on the north road, a pounded ribbon of gravel cut into the mountains, wide enough for one truck. The road took traffic in both directions, but the locals called it the north road because nothing of value or good travelled to the south.

We climbed and descended the road's narrow switchbacks. We passed over endless ridges and found ourselves standing in the shadow of a long valley. We stopped here, heaving and sweating from our journey. This was our rifle range.

Naseeb drove a white binjo ahead of us. He parked next to a shipping container that had been left on the range. He now worked at a large combination lock bolted to its front. The metal shackle popped loose. He walked inside.

Issaq shouted: What are you waiting for! Get in line! Get in line!

We lined up. Naseeb handed each of us an old bolt-action rifle, British Lee-Enfields and German Mausers. The weapons were in poor condition. Their wood hand guards had petrified, their stocks were chipped and some of their barrels bent. The best rifles, Kalashnikovs, were saved for the soldiers, not us recruits. And a man, even a recruit, cannot separate his worth from his rifle's.

All morning we shot from the valley floor, our targets the rocks and the trees. We grasped the steel globe on the bolt handle's end. We levered it up, sliding the bolt back, opening the rifle's breech. Into it, we placed fat, old bullets, their cartridges dented, their once sharp slugs worn down to lead nubs. We fired from every position – sitting, kneeling, lying down, walking, running. Whether or not our bullets hit anything appeared to be of little interest to Issaq. He seemed to care only that we followed his instructions. Most of the time I was too frightened to fire in case I missed badly. I only pretended to shoot.

At midday Naseeb brought us lunch. We could hear the wheels on his white binjo scrape its chassis every time he hit a bump. He parked next to our firing line and stepped outside. I smiled at him and he at me, but when Issaq marched towards him, he turned quickly to his duties.

What have you brought for me today, my fat friend? Issaq asked.

Naseeb nodded towards the passenger seat.

Issaq lifted a thermos from the binjo and inhaled its steaming contents. Ah! Excellent! And for them? he asked.

Yes, yes, the usual, said Naseeb.

Serve it up, Issaq told him. Then he sat with his lunch in the shade of the trees and forgot us. Naseeb pulled two black trash bags from the trunk. Our squad formed a broken line next to him. Inside one bag was leftover naan from the soldiers' mess, in the other raw white onions. The cursing began, just soft enough so Issaq couldn't hear it.

Not again.

Bowli, Piss.

How can we fight on these rations! shouted someone.

This met with many grunts of approval.

Stop your whining! interrupted Mortaza, the season's first recruit, who'd endured this existence longer than any. There is plenty to eat, he scolded. Whether it's good is no matter.

I took my meal and sat next to Tawas and his brother Qiam. Most of the squad could grow at least the wisps of a beard. Like me, these two couldn't yet. Unlike the others, the brothers laughed as they ate.

This is a feast, said Qiam. Such luck we recruits have!

The onions are a little undercooked, but the naan more than makes up for it, replied Tawas from under his sandy brown curls.

The black-haired brother, Qiam, smacked me on the back and asked: How about you, my friend? Any recommendations for the chef?

Not knowing how to answer, I was silent.

Qiam shrugged the bony knobs of his shoulders. He gave me a hard stare as though perhaps my silence were an insult. Tawas grinned and grabbed his brother by the elbow. Ah, a mute! he said, looking at me. He is perfect!

Some branches thrashed above us as Mortaza climbed a pine tree. Brown needles rained down as he brushed against them. He separated himself from the squad, leaning along a thick limb to eat. He watched over the brothers, and me, and the other soldiers who grumbled.

We finished the naan and onions, and were full enough. Our training resumed. When the sun broke the ridgeline, Issaq hiked us back to the firebase for dinner. We always had training at night so we kept our rifles during the meal. This was important. Dinner was the only time we'd see the nearly thirty soldiers of the Special Lashkar. To possess a rifle was the only connection we recruits had to them. I envied their uniforms and learned to hate the loose shalwar kameez I'd worn all my life.

At dinner we ate well, a korma of stewed beef or goat, the meat loose and tender, and rice baked with oil, salt, and butter in the style of a chalow. We sat almost as equals with the soldiers of the mess. Not trusting us, they said little about the fighting season to come. Instead they'd remember old friends, laughing at stories from years before. Weeks passed, and the winter wore on. We suffered its depths. The more the other soldiers saw us, ragged and bleary-eyed, tromping into the mess, the less guarded their words became.

Not long before spring, Gazan's men set off another bomb in Orgun. It destroyed the ground floor of a building where Ali and I used to beg. Six people had died. The soldiers spoke of it openly. They wondered how Commander Sabir would respond. Gazan was said to be hiding in the hills south of Shkin, in a stretch of isolated border villages. The Americans wanted Gazan captured or killed. Mr Jack would supply Commander Sabir well to go after him, delivering new rifles and uniforms, and, it was whispered, increasing the Special Lashkar's budget for this next fighting season. Each night at dinner, we learned more of what was to come. This meal and the morsels of information we gathered gave us the energy and patience to endure the torments of our training.

Issaq always ate in the corner at a small table with the other squad and team leaders. At its head, Commander Sabir leaned back in his chair, his arms folded across his slender body, staring at his food like a contract's fine print. Now and then he chewed a mouthful, his face clamping into a resentful look, as if he wished he relied on nothing for nourishment.

Passage to Commander Sabir's small table was through achievements in combat. He wore this violent reminder across his disfigured face. He had a mangled bottom lip. It looked like the blown-out end of a firecracker. Behind it, rows of teeth, some gold, some rotted, some still white, stuck out at the world with an underbite and snarl. This disfigurement, as well as the scars, paunches, and calluses of the other men gave the group an honest authority, one greater than shining medals and rank.

After dinner the night unfolded just like the afternoon except that Issaq met us with his motorcycle and wore a helmet with night-vision goggles. None of us had night vision and we struggled and scraped to keep up with him as he puttered back to the range. Heaving and sweating, we arrived and began our work, firing through our bolt-action Lee-Enfields and Mausers, their barrels bent, and missing our targets always. In the cold night the steam from our warm bodies rose and mixed with the smoke of our shots, covering the range in a haze. My mind wandered, and with it the haze seemed to clear – my mother's secret, her brown and green eyes, my father's rifle hidden in the woodpile, what Gazan took from Ali – it all appeared vividly. My life as a soldier loomed, though, the haze returning. That winter, had I seen the future as clearly as the past, I might have run away.

Eventually the days became warm. In the mountains the needles on the pines thickened and we knew spring would soon arrive. After a while longer the nights became warm too. On one warm night we returned from the range and each of us had a fresh green uniform waiting on our blanket. The next morning Issaq didn't come for us, Commander Sabir did.

II

OUTSIDE THE BARRACKS we lined up in two rows for our final inspection. Mortaza stood in front. He was most senior among us. This was a very little thing, but Mortaza was proud and so were we. Our new uniforms rested stiffly on our bodies, whose muscle, sinew, and bone were knotted more tightly after the weeks of training.

Commander Sabir wore the same uniform, but his was faded and soft. He carried it with an ease, as though he were the first person ever to put on a uniform. He approached us. Issaq attached himself to his shoulder, desperately speaking some last point. Commander Sabir nodded patiently at his boots as they walked. Issaq was still talking as Commander Sabir planted himself in front of Mortaza. Then he silenced Issaq just loud enough for us all to hear: Yes, yes old friend, but you've done your job well and they are ready.

Commander Sabir grasped Mortaza by the arm. Mortaza threw up his narrow chest in an effort to fill his uniform. You have been here the longest, said Commander Sabir. I remember when you arrived in the fall, just as the weather turned. You almost left when we said you'd have to train all winter. Now summer is here. When the weather turns again, Gazan will know the suffering he caused your family.

With these words, Mortaza tensed the weave of muscles in his arms and legs as if wrestling down some part of himself. Commander Sabir stepped away. He moved through our ranks, finding Tawas and Qiam, who were unable to stop glancing down at their oversized uniforms, worn like clothing from a season they'd yet to grow into. Ah, the two brothers Taqbir discovered destitute in the north, he said. Who would call you orphans now?

When one family is taken, God provides another, said Qiam.

So he does, said Commander Sabir.

His broken mouth unrolled into a grin that was almost a snarl. He moved through our formation, speaking the name of each soldier and some fact about him, usually the injury or insult that led him to the Special Lashkar. Then he came to me, gripping my shoulder as he spoke for all to hear: Aziz from the bazaar in Orgun, your brother, once strong, is now a legless cripple, another of Gazan's victims. Your badal should be feared.

Commander Sabir swept his eyes over the entire squad. Gazan and his Taliban thugs will fear all of you! he said. Then he leaned in close and grabbed the back of my neck. He whispered: Ali is well. Taqbir has recently visited him. He assures me of it and will bring more news soon.

Since I'd arrived at the firebase I hadn't mentioned Ali to anyone. But the way Commander Sabir looked at me — his set jaw, his convincing eyes — I felt certain he'd learned every detail, even the worst one, which he didn't speak of. We soldiers stood proudly in front of him, our chests out and heads back. He offered his ugly smile to each of us as though we were his dearest children. And we felt it to be true.

After Commander Sabir finished his inspection, we were spread between the two thirteen-man squads of the Special Lashkar known as the Comanches and Tomahawks. Issaq pulled a list from his pocket and read our assignments: Aziz, Tomahawk! And so too were Mortaza and Tawas. He continued down his list: Qiam, Comanche! The brothers gave each other a pleading look, never having imagined that they could be separated. Issaq finished reading the rest of the squad's assignments. He returned his list to his pocket and made his final announcement: Batoor is the leader of the Comanches. I am the leader of the Tomahawks.

I turned towards Mortaza. He gave me a look as desperate as the one exchanged between Qiam and Tawas. Without recruits to train, Issaq was free to lead our squad.

For the rest of the morning we followed Naseeb around the firebase. From his containers he issued the items that made us soldiers -- Kalashnikovs, helmets, night-vision goggles, and body armour with steel plates for the chest and back. Mortaza, Tawas, and I then moved from our HESCO barracks to a plywood hut, the barracks of the Tomahawks. Inside it was empty. The rest of the squad had hiked out to the rifle range and wouldn't return until lunch. Rows of wooden beds ran the length of the barracks. On top of every one was a foam mattress. Mine was so thin that I soon learned the pattern of nailheads in the bed planks by how they pressed into my back as I slept. Already our blankets and sheets had been made up. Printed on them were cartoon characters I'd never seen but would soon know – GI Joe, SpongeBob SquarePants, Masters of the Universe, and others. Later Naseeb would tell me how he'd stolen three pallets of this bedding off the runway at FOB Sharana. It'd belonged to a Christian charity, he'd said.

Silently we unpacked. Settling was not a matter of moving our belongings, but of the other soldiers' accepting us. That challenge would begin when they returned. Until then we sat on the edge of our beds. Free time was a luxury we'd forgotten how to use, so we did and said nothing. The quiet lasted until the barracks' door swung open, and the Tomahawks charged inside, their faces full of sweat and their mouths full of profanity.

Khar! shouted one soldier. I told you the barrel was worn!

Who has the extra batteries for our night vision? complained another.

What do you think that fat shit Naseeb will have for dinner tonight?

On it went as one by one they filled the barracks and heaved off their body armour. Last to enter the long open bay was Yar, the second team leader of the squad. Where the others moved fast, he stood out in his slowness. His right pinky and ring finger were missing, and while the rest of the Tomahawks stripped off their equipment and chattered wildly, he unfastened his buckles and straps with a measured effort. I never learned how he lost the fingers. I heard he came to the Special Lashkar with them missing and I imagined his reason for being here was in the story of his disfigured hand. With only three fingers, the hand looked like a rooster's talon. Although his talon made him slower than the others, it also made him focus his energies on simple tasks. Perhaps this is why he was the last into the barracks but the first to notice our group in the back corner. He considered us without acknowledgement. Set in his eyes was a tired heaviness. The skin beneath them was like an orange peel, rough and smooth both at once. He unclasped his helmet and it revealed a full mane of salt-and-pepper curls.

These are my new ones? he asked Issaq, who'd just entered the barracks as well.

Issaq nodded. They're yours, he replied.

Yar stepped in front of us, his right hand extended. Welcome, is all he said.

He took us across the firebase's dusty courtyard to the mess hall. Inside we filled our trays with chalow, naan, and a korma. We sat together and Yar ate in spurts and spoke in bullets as though he were going down a list: Issaq is a hard but good man, fearless in combat. Do not think ill of him because of your training. He stuffed his mouth with the naan and said: The summer will be bloody. With you all, we have many fighters and weapons, but so too does Gazan. Yar guzzled a half can of Fanta and continued: We hear Gazan is hiding in the mountains near Gomal, a small border village south of here. Commander Sabir wants to build an outpost above the village. He picked a cube of meat out of the korma and threw it in his mouth, speaking as he chewed: The spingaris, elders, in Gomal don't support the idea. They worry it will worsen the fighting. One by one, he licked grease off his fingers. It will be hard to make them agree, he said. He grabbed a toothpick and cranked it in the back of his mouth. His last words, he spoke firmly: But we have many guns and fighters. They will agree.

And when do you think we will begin our raids? asked Mortaza.

You want to run to the guns, eh? said Yar.

Mortaza nodded, sheepishly.

Yar ploughed the fingers of his good hand through his thick, greying hair. No need to run, he said. They'll find you. First we patrol. If you want to kill you have to hunt. Issaq doesn't teach the recruits much, does he? But our next mission is a good one, hard but good. Commander Sabir wants to have a shura in Gomal to speak about the outpost. He knows a smugglers' route that we'll take there. It will make the journey longer, but we can't be seen on the way down. If the spingaris are warned we're coming, they'll leave Gomal to keep from the shura. We'll take the north road back, though. And Tawas, the Comanches are coming too.

Tawas grinned. If the Comanches were coming, so was Qiam.

How long will we be gone? I asked.

Three days, said Yar. What other questions?

We looked back at him, silently, and I think our eyes seemed very open and white.

SIX OF OUR TOYOTA HILUXES lined up so early in the morning that it was still night. The convoy idled. Engines warmed the darkness with their invisible hum. Loose-jointed doors, tailgates, and hoods rattled. Each truck was ten, maybe fifteen years old. The Americans could have given us better, but they chose not to. Like each of us, the HiLux was an economical choice, and usually reliable. Our squad was divided between two trucks. One led by Issaq, the other by Yar. Mortaza, Tawas, and I rode with Yar. Through my night-vision goggles the convoy glowed like the many green parts of a caterpillar, easing forwards and back, readying to move. I perched on a pair of ammunition cans in the bed of our pickup. Standing behind the roll bars, I manned our machine gun. Nervously clutching its pistol grip, I felt anxious for my first trip to the southern mountains. I watched the drivers run up and down the convoy, making their last-minute checks. It'd be two days down the smugglers' route, a half day for the shura, and then only a few hours to return on the north road. Three days.

Up front, Commander Sabir's HiLux shifted into gear. Each side of its hood bore a small black, green, and red Afghan flag. The flags caught the wind and his truck looked as though it belonged in Karzai's motorcade. Attached to the long antenna on his tailgate was an infrared chem-light. It bounced overhead, keeping rhythm with the night like a finger taps a beat to music, and the convoy drove out the gate and onto the hard-packed north road. Behind Commander Sabir came Issaq's truck and then ours. Trailing us were the Comanches, who marked their doors with two red vertical stripes. Our doors had one. Mr Jack called this our war paint. He had a great affection for the American West. He thought we Afghans did not understand what it meant to be named after the Indians of his country, but we understood. To us, it seemed a small but misguided sort of insult. For our tribes had never been conquered.

As the truck gained speed, my machine gun swung from its swivel, threatening to strike me. I held its buttstock. We accelerated and the cold air spilled down my shirt and crawled up my pant legs, sticking to me. I tucked my chin into my waterproof jacket and grimaced with envy past the window where Mortaza, Tawas, and Yar sat in the heated cab. Through my many layers of clothing, I struggled to keep my ass from falling off its narrow perch. Every few minutes the HiLux bounced hard and slammed me into the bed as it went over a rut or hole. I kept my body stiff and ready for impact at all times. I felt like a boxer absorbing blows, round after round.

We rushed past Shkin village, where cooking fires glowed inside the few mud-walled homes. We drove on towards the darkness of the southern mountains. At the base of the range, our convoy slowed to a crawl. Here the north road continued south, but we turned off and traversed the uneven ground to a wet ravine that rolled out like a sloppy tongue. I watched Commander Sabir's HiLux ease itself into the ravine's mouth. It took the first bend and was swallowed by the mountain.

Issaq's HiLux followed and then, quickly, the rest of us. And our convoy disappeared.

The mountains closed around us. We drove through them like children playing in a window's long curtains, chasing each other, all of us near, but hidden in the folds. The route was narrow and dangerous. We were defenceless. Our gamble was that no one would find us. Hours passed. We walked alongside our trucks as they struggled to cross the shale-covered slopes. We shuffled into the flooded floor of the ravine, soaked and frozen to the chest, testing its depth before fording with the vehicles.

By late morning it seemed that Commander Sabir's gamble had paid off. Since entering the mountains, we hadn't seen a soul. If our luck held, we'd reach Gomal the next day. Into the afternoon we crept along the ravine. The bed of our pickup rocked me to sleep and the sky was of the sharpest blue, one I felt on the back of my eyelids.

Suddenly our convoy stopped. We sat with our engines idling. I soon grew bored. I jumped from the bed and ran towards the lead truck to see what was going on. Yar watched me go, reclining his seat as I passed so he might rest awhile.

A pool of water had collected in the ravine. Commander Sabir's HiLux had crossed through its shallow end, but Issaq's driver had chosen to make his own path and he was stuck in the deep water. Another HiLux raced up from the back of the convoy. The mechanic. His truck crossed the pool and stopped on its far side. A short man who fit easily under a hood, the mechanic desperately fastened and unfastened a tow strap to the fender of Issaq's stranded HiLux. Both trucks revved their engines, straining without success. Issaq stood by the side of the floodwaters, arms crossed, a scowl plastered to his face, doing nothing.

I perched myself along the side of a hill and leaned against a pine. Looking down, I felt very smug thinking of the many ways I could lie in ambush and kill us all.

Spey zoy! What's wrong with you? shouted Issaq to his driver.

The driver frantically cycled through each gear. First to second, second to third, third to fourth – mud and steam frothed up from the submerged exhaust. On the far side of the pool the mechanic's HiLux groaned, its tow strap twisting and stretching.

Commander Sabir's HiLux came back around one of the range's rocky fingers, its two flags flapping softly. He hopped out just as his front tyres hit the far edge of the water. His truck crossed the pool without him, coming to a stop behind Issaq's on the near bank. Commander Sabir waded, waist deep, into the frigid water. His face was calm and his thighs rose above the surface with his steps.

The driver's eyes bulged as he saw Commander Sabir coming for him. Again he flailed through the gears and revved the engine. Again hot mud and steam spat up from below.

When Commander Sabir got within earshot of the stranded HiLux, he cursed from his stomach's depths with words I couldn't understand. His curses stopped the noise of grinding gears. Silence pierced the ravine. The driver remained in the cab, unmoving, cemented in his seat by fear. Commander Sabir continued to plod through the water like a thick-chested horse. He pulled himself onto the truck's running boards, surveyed the pool, and then shot his fist into the cab's open window, crushing the driver's nose. The flat crunch of it echoed down the ravine, but the driver didn't call out.

Commander Sabir opened the door from the inside, grabbed him by the shirt, and threw him into the pool. A slow thread of blood mixed with the water's brine, forming a long grey streak.

Commander Sabir sat in the driver's seat and waved back to his HiLux.

The flags on the hood playfully caught the wind as it sped towards the stranded truck. I couldn't believe what I was about to see, but in the instant before the crash, Commander Sabir popped the clutch. Like a wounded animal making a final push for life, the stranded truck shuddered forwards. The collision plus the shudder was enough to knock the truck up into the shallow water, and it drove under its own power to the far side of the pool.

Commander Sabir stepped from the cab. His driver passed him a handheld radio. He barked some commands into it. He then walked over to the broken-nosed driver, waved a finger in his face, and patted him on the shoulder. The problem solved, Commander Sabir climbed into his HiLux and drove back to the convoy's front.

He left the driver standing next to Issaq and their mud-soaked truck. Before either could climb in, a three-seated military van we called an asses-three — only later did I learn it was called this because its Red Army designation had been AS-3 — arrived from the back of the convoy. It was the ambulance, its red sickle moon scrawled into the rear double doors with a paint pen. A round and sleepy-eyed medic climbed from out the back. He pushed gauze into the driver's face.

How did you break your nose? he asked.

The driver said nothing.

*

Deeper and deeper we crawled into the ravine, but we couldn't measure our progress. Each turn revealed yet another. We hid ourselves in the mountains' folds so not even it knew we were there. We didn't see the sun except for the midday hour when it made its slow leap across the sliver of sky that parted the ravine's two walls. The day eased into a damp afternoon shade and out of the ground rose a cold and a darkness that stuck.

We drove until our convoy stopped without warning. The engines that had rumbled so long I barely heard them died. A silence, which seemed louder, replaced their noise. Yar stepped out of the cab. Resting his hands against his hips, he leaned back and groaned. Aziz, he said, give Mortaza your machine gun. He'll take the first shift. Come in. Warm up.

Mortaza climbed out of the cab and put on every piece of clothing he owned. He stood below me, his arms outstretched. I passed him the heavy-barrelled gun and he cradled it like too much firewood. Before he could say anything, I jumped into the cab of our HiLux. I shut the door and leaned against it. I pulled up the hood of my waterproof jacket and tugged the drawstring tight, covering my face. Exhaustion shot up my legs and into my back.

I fell asleep.

It was the type of sleep that came and went like a thunderclap. Late in the night, when Mortaza opened the door of the cab, my body jerked awake. I nearly fell into the dirt. My turn on security. I stiffly unfolded my legs into the biting air. Moon shade fell in patches across the pine-covered mountains. Mortaza wedged himself into my warm seat and slammed the door behind him. He'd left the machine gun in the dirt. I yoked its awkward metal edges across my shoulders and climbed to my post on the high ground. I grabbed onto branches and trunks to pull myself up the steep incline. The cold sap under the tree bark stuck to my hands, smelling sweet. In the ravine below, the moon glimmered off the many windshields of the convoy, its light strung like pearls. I continued through the high forest, to the bald summit above still covered in snow. Here, I could see the dark silhouette of the Comanches' sentry one ridgeline over. He leaned against a pine and stamped his feet to keep warm. The wind howled over the rough-cut peaks. My post had no trees to block it. I huddled against a knee-high rock wall Mortaza had built. I searched to the south, towards Gomal, for any danger. I saw only the unending summits and ravines that spread in all directions, threatening to swallow us. Against the wall I sat, freezing and alone.

My senses dulled. Time passed. How much I couldn't say. Then a rock slipped below me, and several after it. I scrambled to the crest of the ridge, looking down, to where Yar struggled on all fours to find his footing. He called up to me: Good, you are awake and alert. His words fell against the unyielding wind. He climbed the last few steps to join me. He winced at the cold. We built the rock wall a little wider so he could fit behind it. We sat next to each other, and having a warm shoulder against mine was a great improvement. I hoped Yar would stay for a while.

These mountains are tough driving, I said.

Very tough, he answered. He tucked his chin into his jacket. His greying curls fell from under his wool cap, blown back by the wind.

Do you think we'll arrive in Gomal tomorrow? I asked.

Of course, he muttered into his collar.

What if tomorrow's driving is worse than today's?

Yar lifted his head from his jacket: We'll make it.

How can you be sure?

Yar looked as though I'd asked how he could be certain that the unseen wind whipping across the ridge was real. He gazed south to the carpet of mountains we'd cross tomorrow. I trust Commander Sabir, he said as if in a prayer. He will get us there. Then he pushed himself from the wall and held my eyes with his. He added: This will be my fourth fighting season with him. I know him. It is because I know him that I trust him. I trust him with my life. Yar settled next to the wall again. He leaned heavily against it. His thick arms warmly pushed against mine. He asked: What do you know?

I said nothing.

Commander Sabir's brother used to lead the Special Lashkar. Did you know this? he asked, wanting an answer.

No, I didn't.

Yes, many years ago, he said. Only the old hands like me remember. Commander Sabir's brother was Jazeem, but the Americans called him James. They gave him the money to start the Special Lashkar.

I smiled, thinking of an Afghan commander named James.

Is there something about my friend that amuses you? he asked.

The grin swept from my face.

This one was a fearsome fighter, said Yar. Perhaps too much so. He was killed in an ambush not far from here.

What happened? I asked, my voice solemn.

At that time, he said, the militants fought under the Haqqani banner, led by a man named Hafez, a ruthless spizoe, son of a bitch. In Pirkowti, a half day south of Gomal, the spingaris refused to support Hafez and his fighters with food, water, and shelter. Hafez took his men into the mountains around the village. From there they fired mortar barrage after mortar barrage among the homes. This levelled Pirkowti and killed many. The cowards refused to stop unless the spingaris took a vote in the shura to give them the shelter they wanted. The spingaris understood nang. They wouldn't hand over their homes to this dog so they asked Commander James for help. Commander James also understood nang and we went to Pirkowti's defence. But it was a ploy. Along the north road Hafez laid an ambush. First there was a mine. The front truck flipped over and trapped two soldiers inside while it burned. Hafez's fighters pinned us down, firing from the high ridgelines with rifles and RPGs. Commander James would not leave his two soldiers in the road to die and he would not ask others to do what he would not do himself. He ran into Hafez's guns to save them.

Yar shook his head and tucked his chin back into his jacket. His next words came as a mumble: He never made it to the truck.

And the two soldiers? I asked.

He looked at me. His words were clear: We watched them burn.

I leaned my chest into my knees. The wind kept coming.

Commander James's family was left very poor, he said. Soon Commander Sabir joined us as a regular soldier to support them. For a time, Issaq, Batoor, and even some of the team leaders led the Special Lashkar. There was great uncertainty in our ranks and much infighting. No one was an adequate replacement. But Commander Sabir began to prove himself. Many said he possessed the same ferocity as his brother. He was promoted to team leader under Batoor, but just as the fighting season was ending, he disappeared for a month. Some said he'd lost his nerve and deserted. They said, perhaps there is less of Commander James in him than we thought. But one morning at the end of that month, he arrived at the firebase's front gate. I saw him as he returned. The guards didn't recognise him, for his face was unrecognisable. The wound on his lip was still fresh.

It wasn't the torn lip alone that made him look different. His eyes seemed darker. Not as if their colour had changed, but as if they'd looked at some black and faraway thing, absorbing it. Soon the news spread among every soldier that Commander Sabir had taken his badal. He'd tracked down Hafez and killed him in the mountains. How, I still don't know, but after that he commanded.

The wind stopped. The sky was quiet. We sat on a ridgeline that ran to the south, to where Commander James had died with his nang and to the unknown place where Commander Sabir had killed Hafez.

Yar stood. With his good hand, he brushed the dirt from the seat of his pants. He looked at our convoy that sat cold and sleeping below. He breathed deeply and said: We'll reach our destination tomorrow.

＊

Gomal sat naked and ugly in the dust. The moon was up. It was late on the second night and we'd arrived on schedule. Our column rushed forwards and split in half. The Comanches surrounded the hilltops. The rest of us accelerated sharp and straight into the village. We sifted through its dusty streets and a maze of compounds rose around us, filling the narrow valley. The high mud walls of the houses, each its own fortress, trapped us, threatening violence from their unseen courtyards. We parked in a square bazaar lined with shuttered storefronts and bare stalls. Our squad's two HiLuxes flanked Commander Sabir's, which idled in the bazaar's centre.

From the driver's seat Yar stepped out, rifle in hand. I'm going to see about the plan, he said. Wait here. And he walked towards the other trucks. I stood, stretching my back and legs. Around us, the villagers shuffled behind compound walls. Dogs howled from the roofs of the mud houses. Woodsmoke streamed dark and green through my night-vision goggles, rising lazily in the sky as one by one breakfast fires, theirs and ours, were lit.

Tawas and Mortaza left the cab and gathered around the hood of our HiLux. Aziz, what's the matter? asked Mortaza. You look cold.

Bacha bazi, I cursed.

He laughed and said: You know, the heater inside was so strong during the drive I thought of taking your place, just to cool off.

I spat at Mortaza's feet. Again he laughed.

Tawas asked if I wanted some milk tea. Crouching by our HiLux's front tyre, he raised a small blue flame from our propane stove. He smacked bubblegum as he brewed the leaves in a pot. I leaned over my machine gun, staring down at him.

Where did you get that? I asked, pointing to his mouth.

He smiled back at me. His lips and teeth were blue, as if he'd sipped from an inkwell. Naseeb sold me two large boxes' worth, he answered. Steam rose from the pot's spout. Tawas poured me a cup of the milk tea. He brought it and a stick of his gum to the HiLux's bed, where I stood behind the machine gun. He and I chewed our gum, drank from our mugs, and looked out to the dark compound walls.

He spoke softly: Gomal reminds me of the village where Qiam and I lived as boys.

My mind wandered back to Sperkai and that morning years ago, when I'd last seen my mother and father. I thought of Ali, how he'd held me up in the tree when I'd tried to climb down. I looked to the ridgelines that surrounded us. Surely someone was up there, hiding and watching. Perhaps it was Gazan and his fighters, or perhaps some frightened boys wondering what we'd do to their homes.

This seems a tough place to live, I said to Tawas.

He folded his arms and hung them over the side of the bed. These people have nothing, he said. They are ignorant even of their suffering. This is the worst poverty.

Mortaza leaned against the hood of the HiLux, also sipping his milk tea. Down a dark street, a pair of ragged boys, one a little older than the other, watched him. He watched them too. They crept closer, begging for food, scooping air from their empty hands to their mouths. Mortaza flung the tea from his mug at them. They ran around the mud wall of the nearest house, peeking back at Mortaza while he refilled his mug. Tawas called out after the boys, holding up two sticks of his gum. The boys stuck their heads around the wall. Slowly they crept closer. Tawas held up a third stick, tossed the foil wrapper into the dirt, and chewed it. The two boys, understanding what was being offered, ran up to Tawas and snatched the gum from his hand. They scrambled back towards the mud wall. After only a few steps the littlest boy turned around. He ran back and scooped up the piece of foil Tawas had thrown into the dirt.

Mortaza snorted at Tawas: Why should you feel pity for them?

Because they are like me, he said.

They are not like you. You've done something to lift yourself up. These people do nothing.

Who are you to make that judgement? asked Tawas.

Judgement? This is no judgement. Open your eyes. Their indifference stares back at you. It is in their mud houses, overfilled sewers, and dirtfaced children who are stupid and unknowing.

64

It is only right to help them escape that, I said.

Yes, help them, he replied, but not with charity. Those boys will spend this whole day watching you, hoping for another stick of gum, instead of working for the meal that could fill their stomachs.

You didn't come from a village like this, said Tawas. That's why you say such things.

I have known death and loss just as you, Mortaza said. I have suffered. Those boys need an example of strength. The promise of charity has paralysed them. Our charity, the Americans' charity – I pray God delivers them from charity.

Mortaza threw the rest of his milk tea into the dirt. He walked around the front of our HiLux and sat alone in the driver's seat. Soon morning light brushed the ridges. At the peaks the rock yielded its shadow to colour, but in the heights the sky remained black and for a time the stars could be seen along with the first of the sun. The three of us watched the sky, but also the rooftops as the dark silhouettes of the villagers gathered to look down on us.

Yar returned with fresh orders. Mortaza, Aziz, he said, come, there's work to do. We assembled around him, and he told us: You two wake the spingaris, elders, of each house. Let them know that in an hour they are to be in the bazaar for the shura.

I jumped down from the bed and grabbed my rifle. Mortaza fastened the chin strap on his helmet. Tawas interrupted our departure. This is not how a meelma, a guest, behaves, he told Yar.

This is how a soldier behaves, Yar answered back. He turned to Mortaza and me. Go! he snapped.

Not wishing to wake anyone, we first went to the homes where smoke already curled up from the chimneys. Still, a scowl met us at every door. Assent to our request was given with a grunt or a nod. Soon every chimney billowed smoke and all of Gomal was awake.

The last house we visited was on the village's edge, among the border's first low hills. It didn't have a chimney and the outer wall was made of concrete, not of mud, and a satellite dish extended from its roof. Mortaza banged on its red steel gate with the heel of his boot. There was an expectant clunk and the gate slid open. A man with smooth olive skin greeted us. This was Atal, an important spingari I'd come to know well. His dress was neat and his body perfumed so heavily that his scent caused in me a spinning moment of drunkenness. He extended his hand as though we should kiss it.

Salaam, may I help you? he asked.

His turban was bright orange and his shalwar kameez an emerald green, matching his eyes, which were flecked in many places. Beneath his two-fist beard hung a tear-shaped opal on a chain of braided silver. The kind of necklace a woman would wear. Around his neck the feminine trace suggested a cunning and manly ferocity.

Salaam, I said. We are here with—

Atal interrupted: Ah, well, I've forgotten my hospitality. Please come in, you must be hungry, join me.

He shook our hands as we entered. His touch left my palm oiled and smooth. We crossed the outer wall and walked towards the main house. Parked in the courtyard was the same-model Toyota HiLux the Americans supplied to us. But unlike ours, which were painted grey to match the mountain rock, his bore a civilian paint scheme, white with a pronounced silver lightning bolt down its side. A generator hummed in the compound's far corner. From it, insulated wires ran in a tangle to the main house. In the living room a heater blew, and carpets covered tiled floors while plush sofas lined the walls. In the corner an enormous Hitachi television leaned against the ground. I could hear low murmurs of Urdu as programmes from Pakistan flashed across its plasma screen.

Please, sit, sit, said Atal.

I unlaced my muddy boots so I wouldn't dirty his carpet. He gave me an appreciative nod, but Mortaza shot me a hard glance. I tied them back on. Soldiers don't lounge around in their stocking feet. We sat across from Atal, and he stretched himself elegantly along one of the sofas. Between thumb and forefinger, he spun the opal that hung around his neck and pushed his chest up, leaning towards the back of the house.

Fareeda! he shouted. Bring breakfast, child. We have guests.

A clanging and shuffling came from the kitchen in back. Atal lazily rolled his head towards us. His expression was so relaxed it offered more warmth than had he smiled. I apologise, he said. My niece would've already prepared something had I known of your visit, but I am very pleased to have guests. You have come here with Sabir, no? I trust he is well. Please offer him my warmest regards.

Mortaza nodded. He sat on the sofa's edge and leaned forwards, tensely, his elbows perched against his knees. Commander Sabir is holding a shura in the bazaar, he said. The head of every household is asked to attend.

Ah, yes, please send him my apologies, but I have other business today.

Mortaza leaned further over his elbows, repeating himself: Commander Sabir requests the head of every household.

A young woman, still girl enough to go without a burka at home among strangers, emerged from the kitchen. She struggled to carry a heavy silver tray crowded with glasses of milk tea and honey cakes. She hoisted it high above her head, using only her left arm. She set the first glass in front of Atal, who kissed his teeth at her and waved the back of his hand so that we, his guests, would be served first. She nodded and looked at Atal kindly. Her hijab sat loosely over her head, she'd yet to wrap it properly, and her smooth black hair spilled from its edges like a sheet of oil. Her eyes held many colours, never catching light the same way twice. Flecks of emerald and black, and a deep uncut red turned orbits in her stare. I could tell you that the mixing of all this colour resulted in brown, and it did, but in her eyes brown was no more a single colour than in two palms filled with rare stones. She kneeled down and one by one set out glass mugs filled with milk tea, a shade of earth like clay. She placed small round honey cakes on little plates. Her movements were quick and all made with her left hand. Over her shoulder she wore a bright blue shawl and beneath it her right arm hung limply by her side. She picked up the tray and tucked it under her left arm. As she did, I saw the right hand. It was grotesque, the thumb and index finger engorged as though they were about to burst, the fingernails yellow and brittle. A scrawl of blue veins ran up the hand's back like a sick tree's roots running out from the earth. The sweet scent of her hung around us, and despite her deformity she was lovely. Her beauty rested in the savage contradictions of her body.

Thank you, Fareeda, said Atal. He grabbed her good hand and kissed it.

I will be in the back if you need me, Uncle.

As she spoke, her smile rested on him. Then she turned towards us. Atal sat up on the couch and leaned over his tea.

He grasped a honey cake and locked our eyes in his. He would not allow us to steal anything of her with our glances. She left the room.

We ate and drank silently. Then Mortaza spoke again: Commander Sabir must see all the spingaris. You may need to postpone your business.

Sabir may choose to have business with me, said Atal, but I can choose to have none with him.

We have driven two days and endured much to be here, said Mortaza.

Then I am sorry Sabir drove you for two days to be here, but still I have no business with him.

Our journey means nothing to you?

I interrupted Mortaza: It is enough.

Atal glanced towards me. Then he held Mortaza firmly in his stare. I know why Sabir is here, he said. He knows my position on the matter he'll address at the shura. Send him my regards I imagine it won't be long before I see him.

Mortaza looked away and relented with a nod.

Atal smiled and continued: Now as I said, I have business to attend to and must ask you both to leave. But please, before you go, finish your breakfast.

He stood, bowed lightly, and stepped from the room.

Mortaza and I took a few last bites of food. When we walked into the courtyard, Atal's HiLux was gone. From the back of the house, I saw little clouds of smoke rising. Gazing at them, I asked: What do you think that is?

No trouble of ours, replied Mortaza.

Hold on, I said.

Come, the shura will begin soon!

Go ahead, I called back. I'll be behind you.

He left and I went after the smoke. First I looked to the generator, but it hummed without interruption. Then I saw Fareeda. She lay on a reed mat outside the back door and her head rested on a pair of felt pillows. She rolled on her side, towards a lamp, and dipped the bowl of a pipe into its open flame. As she exhaled she looked at me and her face blurred in a cloud of smoke.

Keana, she said, inviting me to stay. Her head bobbed as I sat next to her. Her arm was laid out on the mat. As she inhaled more smoke, she massaged her knotted flesh. Her strong fingers pressed, the knuckles whitening. Her eyes shut. Mine froze on her. Excitement moved through me. I thought of my mother's cigarettes hidden in the cradle, how I'd felt watching her take them in the night. Fareeda opened her eyes and saw me looking at the arm. She did not move to conceal it.

The pipe is for my pain, she said.

How often must you smoke?

When I have my medicine, very little.

Do you have it now?

No, she said, but my uncle will soon have more for me.

He is your only family?

I have no family, she said. He is my guardian and, before he was killed, a friend to my father. In that way he is my uncle.

She looked away from me and began to work a black ball of the opium between her fingers. She stuck the tar on a needle and dried it over the lamp. It sizzled very softly. She scraped it off the needle and into her pipe, which rested by her pillows. She pulled her sleeve all the way up to the shoulder and I could see the skin on her body. She shut her eyes and worked her fingers deep into the tissue that bulged like some deformed fruit.

Everyone is very afraid of you, she said.

Her eyes shut. Her head nodded.

Why would you be afraid of me? I asked.

She formed her words slowly: It is they who are afraid, not me.

Her eyes opened. She leaned her pipe back into the flame. The smoke came out of her lungs thick and sweet. I could taste it.

Why aren't you afraid of me? I asked.

She looked at her arm and spoke: I feel only the pain of this.

It has always been this way with you?

She didn't answer my question, but turned the pipe back to the flame and breathed, the tar in it sizzling. Exhaling, she spoke, her words shaping the smoke: Not always. They say there was a time when my flesh didn't struggle against itself. They say the right medicine could cure me. But I have little memory of anything else. To me, it has always been so and I think this will always be the way of it.

Her stare settled on mine and its reds, emeralds, and blacks froze, hanging with the stillness of constellations. She shut her eyes and rolled from her side to her back. Her body lay there, breathing shallowly. There was a low scraping sound as she began to grind her teeth and her arm rested on the mat in a patch of sun. My eyes took everything they wanted of her and I knew I could've taken more. Her indifference invited me to, but I also wanted to lift her up, to bring her with me to our clinic, to Orgun, to the hospital with my brother. I wanted to save her and I wanted to savage her, and in that moment I felt I loved her. So I left her on the pillows and when she woke up, I would be gone.

*

The mountains were set against a morning sky that had almost achieved its full blue. I wove through several mud-walled alleys and arrived at the bazaar where I joined Mortaza. He searched a line of spingaris who waited to enter the shura circle. Commander Sabir, Issaq, and Yar mixed among them. An old man whose face seemed no longer of flesh but of something like earth and stone had cornered Yar. He wagged a twig of a finger at his nose. This was Haji Jan, the oldest of the spingaris. He had the greatest influence on how the shura decided and he spat his words at Yar: You bring fighting and Gazan brings fighting. How are you different? We must show you hospitality, but what type of a meelma injures his host?

Yar put his hand gently on Haji Jan's frail back. He shepherded him towards the others. Come baba, sit, he said. Let us discuss this in the proper way, in the shura.

I am not your old fool of a baba, answered Haji Jan. I've seen more of man's deceit than you, young one. But still, he hobbled towards the circle of spingaris and stiffly lowered himself down, taking his place in the dirt.

Yar raised his one good hand and waved Mortaza and me over. We stepped in front of him. Did you tell everyone? he asked.

Yes, said Mortaza, all will come except for the one man, Atal. He says he has important business elsewhere and that Commander Sabir knows his position.

Issaq approached us and interrupted with a snort: That is what he said?

Mortaza and I nodded.

Important business! Issaq laughed. With us gone, his business is surely back at our firebase selling the secrets of his village to the Americans. Issaq then walked to the centre of the shura and whispered Atal's message to Commander Sabir, who shook his head and spat between his two bottom teeth into the dirt.

In the shura, Commander Sabir stood, unarmed and vulnerable, wearing just his sweat-stained uniform. With great formality, he walked the circle and kissed each spingari on the cheek. His embrace was warm, but like a gas flame lacked fullness. He stood in front of the group with his arms open, palms turned to the sky and began: Bizmullah ir Rahman ir Rahim, in the Name of God, the Compassionate, the Merciful. I am humbled that the leaders of Gomal have come together.

He placed his right hand over his heart and gently bowed.

Today you embrace me as a friend, he said, but I see some who've forgotten our friendship. Scowling at the spingaris, he added: Some who've allowed Gazan's men to launch attacks from this village. What I ask of you is melmastia, the hospitality shown to a friend. Permit us to build an outpost among the mountains that look down on Gomal.

Commander Sabir pointed to the east, towards the border. In the distance a bald gathering of boulders came from between the thick-trunked pines. It commanded the ground over which it stood. He said: We will crown that hilltop with a barricade and guns to fight off Gazan's attacks. Our outpost will once again make you rulers of this village.

The spingaris tugged at their beards and silently absorbed the accusations and the proposal. Finally, a large man heaved himself from the ground. His beard was thick and greying, but not yet fully white. He spoke: I am Mumtaz, I have seen much suffering in these wars. Ask anyone of Mumtaz's suffering and they will tell you.

Then you know the importance of protection, said Commander Sabir.

Mumtaz shook his head: You say you wish to build this outpost to protect us, but Gazan only attacks this village when you are here. You bring the war with you, and if you build an outpost it will never leave.

Now Haji Jan slowly stood as if he were growing from the earth. He addressed the shura and his voice was thick as ash. Mumtaz speaks the truth, he said, slapping the back of one hand into the palm of another as he made his point. Sabir, you say this outpost would make us rulers of our village, but you're ruled by the American who pays you. To accept your help means we'd be ruled in that way too.

Commander Sabir's face turned cold. I am ruled by no one, he said.

There have not been attacks here. Why should there be an outpost? asked Haji Jan.

The shura hummed with approval and nods.

Gazan's thugs have been here. They've launched attacks in the north from here. Commander Sabir was nearly shouting: To do nothing is to support them!

They have been here just as you have, interrupted Mumtaz. We bear you no ill will nor do we bear Gazan ill will.

Then you admit it! said Commander Sabir, pointing his finger at Mumtaz. This village has protected him.

Just as we have you, he answered, and offered you melmastia under the laws of Pashtunwali. You ask too much, Sabir. You and Gazan have your war for your own reasons. Our village respects the privacy of that feud. We ask you to respect the privacy of our homes.

Low grumbles of approval met these words. The shura fell to silence. Mumtaz faced Commander Sabir. The heft of his paunch pushed against his billowy shalwar kameez. His beard ran down his face as immovable as the pines.

The outpost will provide great wealth for those who help,

said Commander Sabir. A few spingaris, including Haji Jan and Mumtaz, found the talk of money to be too much. They walked out of the shura shaking their heads. Commander Sabir called after them: War is coming here. My friendship should not be taken lightly. I am not one you want as an enemy.

Those who remained in the circle tugged their beards, grumbled their consideration, and left, disappearing into their mud-walled homes.

The shura was over.

Issaq trooped through the village and waved his arm in a circle above his head, giving the signal for us to load our vehicles and begin the half-day journey back to Shkin. Mortaza and I jogged to our HiLux, where Tawas waited for us. I wedged myself into the bed. From my perch behind the machine gun, I saw the spingaris gather in their courtyards to discuss the proposal. Far off, I saw the satellite dish on Atal's compound and a thin ribbon of smoke still rising from behind.

You ready! Yar shouted at me from the driver's seat.

I banged on the roof of the cab twice. We lurched into gear. Driving out of Gomal, children stepped from their homes forming into packs. They ran after our convoy. Whether they chased us from the village or wanted to come with us, I couldn't say. Our trucks kicked up a white cloud of dust and their voices rose and then choked to silence in the cloud, but still they came. In front of me, I saw an arm reach from our cab. It was Tawas. He threw handfuls of bubblegum into the air. The foil wrappers glinted in the sun, bright against the dust. The children stopped, fell to their knees, and fought each other over too few pieces.

We returned to the mountains.

★

Commander Sabir never drove the same route twice. He was determined, to the point of obsession, not to be ambushed like his brother had been. And staying alive was a good if inconvenient obsession for a commander to have.

Our convoy had left Gomal just before lunch. The sun hung directly overhead, but the pleasure of its warmth was offset by my nagging hunger. We followed a ravine towards the north road. The pebbles and boulders of its bed were washed and grey in the sun. Our HiLux pitched me backward and forwards. I held the stock of my machine gun to stay upright. We splashed through a flooded bank and a jet of cold water smacked my face. It trickled under my collar and down my back. The wind set into me. That, plus my hunger and the long drive ahead, chiselled away my courage.

Suddenly our convoy stopped. From my pocket, I pulled a piece of naan. The vibrations of our HiLux still rang in my body but slowly seeped out of me towards stillness. I enjoyed the stillness. With it, warmth replaced the wind and I ate. The cold and hunger that gnawed at me eased. Soon I realised how dangerous our situation had become. We sat in the ravine and the mountain rose up straight, so close that I could reach out and touch its granite walls from either side of the bed. I tossed my last mouthful of naan onto the ravine floor. I grabbed the buttstock of my machine gun. I opened its feed tray. Inside the mechanics were clean and oiled. The belt of ammunition sat linked and heavy against the worn metal firing mechanism. Lead into brass, lead into brass. The predictable pattern comforted me. I slammed the feed tray shut. The metal-on-metal snap echoed.

Suddenly we lurched backward and reversed to a slightly wider part of the ravine. From the front of the convoy, Commander

Sabir's HiLux drove around us. The flags on its hood snapped in the wind. Yar leaned his head out the driver's window. He wore a green bandana over his curls. Aziz! he shouted back to me. Keep your eyes open. The Comanches got a truck stuck behind us.

On the side of the machine gun was a small metal charging handle. I pulled it back and then slid it forwards, chambering a round. The machine gun was ready to fire, and I felt ready to fire it. Now only Issaq's HiLux was ahead of us. I couldn't see behind us. I didn't know how much of the convoy was stuck. I shouldered my gun. It felt like a man I didn't know was holding a knife against my bare chest. The stranded vehicle blocked the ravine and left us completely vulnerable. My stomach drew tight as a fist. I scanned the tops of the granite walls. Nothing.

Four explosions rolled in the distance. If there'd been clouds in the sky, the noise would've been mistaken for thunder.

What do you see? shouted Yar from the cab.

An arm of smoke reached upward from the direction of Gomal. Before I could reply, the air cut in half and shook. The rocket. A thunderclap so loud it seemed sound and time tried to divorce one another. Just in front of us, its explosion fountained pebbles from the ravine floor. They sprayed wetly across the hood of our HiLux. Fear's knife slid into my chest. The unknown promise of violence had become known. It was painless.

I pushed my machine gun's buttstock down to strafe the high ridges above. It wouldn't depress far enough. From the back of the bed, it could go no higher than the canyon walls. Ahead of us another tuft of smoke uncoiled in the air. It slammed to the ground – a miss. And a remarkably wide one, nearly fifty yards off target. Yar jumped out of our truck. He threw himself against the wall's face. He started to climb. Confused, Tawas and Mortaza froze and watched. With two of his soldiers behind him,

Issaq ran towards us along the ravine. Follow Yar! he screamed, hugging the sheer face, and climbing with his Kalashnikov slung over his shoulder. To the summit! To the summit! he grunted.

Up the canyon wall, Mortaza followed Issaq, and I followed Mortaza, pulling my machine gun off its mount and slinging its dead weight across my back. Tawas trailed behind me. His eyes were wide and white, his mouth open. His fear of being left in the ravine gripped him more than his fear of the summit. We pressed against the mountain, clawing and pulling at its sides. The rock became a greater enemy than our ambushers who now shot over us, unable to see down the sheer face of the wall. We tugged at tree roots and perched one-legged on toeholds.

Just beneath the summit, Yar, Issaq, and Mortaza gathered along a small ledge. Issaq shouted down to me: The machine gun! I scrambled up to their perch. Tawas and a few others still climbed beneath us. My panicked heart drilled a hole into my chest. I arrived exhausted. Weakly, I unslung the gun's heavy weight from my back. My arms drooped as I cradled it. Crammed body to body on the small ledge, Issaq thumbed towards the summit above our heads.

I nodded.

Issaq and Yar bent down. They held Yar's green bandana and made a stirrup for my feet. I stepped onto it, feeling my knees shake. The stirrup gave a little under my weight. Yar looked past me to Mortaza, who stood, rifle in hand, ready to summit and charge the guns that fired steady overhead. Mortaza looked back. His eyes were large and white. His mouth was open, just as Tawas's had been moments before. Yar nodded to Mortaza. He swallowed and nodded back.

Yar and Issaq exploded with their legs, lifting the ends of the bandana I stood on. I reached above my head with the machine gun and, arms extended, barely cleared the top of the ridge. I sprayed wildly, the recoil of the heavy gun knocking me back until I thought I might topple into the ravine.

Under the cover of my shots, Mortaza charged up the cliff. His legs kicked against the steep loose dirt. Just as he summited, Yar and Issaq dropped the ends of the bandana. I slid back down the face of the wall and toppled onto the ledge. The machine gun knocked me on the helmet. It landed, hot at my feet. I looked up and saw Issaq and Yar following after Mortaza. Overhead was the *pop, pop, pop* of rifles and then the hollow *buzz, buzz* of rounds coming back.

I heaved the machine gun across my back and followed Yar and Issaq. The heavy *crump* of a grenade exploded ahead. Dust flew into my face. I scrambled my last few steps and stood on the summit. Quickly it dropped towards the back slope of the ridge. Just where that slope began, a cloud of deep grey smoke rose from the earth.

Once again I pulled the heavy machine gun off my back. I crouched behind a small boulder that, even in a crouch, covered only my chest. I unfolded the machine gun's bipod and fired into the cloud of smoke, *dunk, dunk, dunk, pause, dunk, dunk, dunk, pause*. I couldn't see anyone.

A *crack, hiss* over my head was the only response, but it seemed to come from a distance.

Hold fire! A shout from somewhere in front of me. Issaq? With shaking hands I canted the machine gun towards the sky. The back of my knuckles grazed its smoking barrel. I smelled the faint odour of my burned skin. One side of my father's ring had melted nearly flat against my finger. Awash with nerves, I'd felt almost nothing. Farther up the summit, Mortaza sprinted from behind a large boulder. He ran towards the grenade's grey smoke. It had thinned in the high mountain breeze. He jumped and disappeared into what looked like a hole. From across the summit Yar, Issaq, and Tawas ran towards Mortaza – *pop, pop*, came from where Mortaza disappeared. I ran towards him, too.

We arrived at a small clearing before the reverse slope fell steeply into another ravine. Below us, Mortaza stood in a chest-high trench. It seeped melted mudwater as a gash seeps pus. Piles of rocks had been stacked on the edge to form a parapet. Flopped over the trench's back lip was a dead man. His brown shalwar kameez was neatly tucked into a cartridge belt with double-wide magazine pouches on each side. He was soaked to his knees, but the rest of him was perfectly composed. The final decoration of his soldier's costume was a tidy bullet hole lodged in his forehead. A red spot set cleanly between brown eyes of the usual sort, remarkable only in their projection of nothing. Issaq flipped the man over. As neat as the bullet hole was in front, the back of his head was a split mess.

We wandered about the littered ridgeline. Scattered around the trench were blankets, a small plastic jug of diesel, and a tin pot with warm uneaten rice stuck to its sides. A bag of uncooked rice, stamped *USAID*, leaned open against the wall of the trench. Mortaza heaved the bag over to Issaq and scratched at his chin, which bulged underneath his tight helmet strap.

These are our supplies, said Mortaza. How do you think Gazan's men got them?

I don't know, said Issaq. I'll speak to Naseeb.

The dead man's bolt-action rifle, a Mauser, lay half submerged in the slit trench. It was beaten and weathered. I picked it up and sighted down its length. Its barrel canted noticeably to the right. Tawas took a piece of bubblegum from his pocket.

He chewed it, calming himself. Still breathing hard, he spoke: These fools would have done better to throw rocks.

No wonder they couldn't hit us, said Mortaza.

I felt a fool for being so afraid during the assault. Whoever ordered this ambush must have known it didn't stand a chance. I said: These rifles are as bad as what we trained with as recruits.

Issaq grasped the stock of the Mauser and took it from me. There are no bad rifles, he replied, only bad marksmen. A good marksman makes compensations. For him even the bent rifle shoots straight. But these rifles are familiar.

A low rumble erupted behind us, ending our conversation. Tawas stood and pointed to several thick white columns of smoke. He spoke the obvious: Gazan's mortars punishing Gomal for our shura.

We made our way to the ravine floor. Each of us was very quiet. We were in awe of how reckless it'd been to throw ourselves against the canyon wall. More mortars fell in the village. By the time we climbed down into the ravine, the thick white columns of smoke had become a black haze that drifted into the mountains around us. Gomal had caught fire.

We arrived back at our trucks. The rest of the convoy was lined up and waiting. Commander Sabir stood with his boot planted against our fender. He clapped each of us on the back as we loaded our HiLux. Good hunting! he said. Good hunting by all. And we smiled the way small men do when they satisfy a great one. Our convoy departed and pulled deeper into the mountains, closer to our firebase, to home. I thought perhaps we would go back to Gomal and help them. But we didn't. I doubt Commander Sabir ever considered it. It was better to let the fires burn.

WHEN MR JACK CAME to our firebase, he came at night. He parked his black HiLux amid our grey ones in the motor pool. Our mechanic knew to wash the truck for him. In the morning, it sat glimmering on the wet gravel. All day we soldiers walked by, each of us finding our reflection in its black door and hood. Mr Jack spent these days in a special building tucked in the perimeter's far corner, just a shack really. We caught passing glimpses of those he met with. They looked unimportant, herders who wandered and saw much in their wanderings or elders from far-off border towns. Once or twice I caught sight of Mr Jack in the day. Always he wore a pair of wraparound sunglasses, their lenses mirrored. Behind them, I imagined his eyes were very blue, the sort I'd seen from afar but never looked into. Once his business was done and before he left, he'd always visit Commander Sabir in his quarters. These visits lasted until late, and we could hear laughter through the walls, the type of late laughter that required a bottle. And this is the way Mr Jack arrived at night and left at night.

A few days after we returned from our patrol, I spotted Mr Jack's HiLux in the motor pool as I walked to breakfast. There was nothing strange in this. What was strange was that Atal's

HiLux was parked next to it. I remembered the way Atal's limp, oiled hand had felt in mine. The idea of him meddling in our affairs unsettled me. My mind and stomach churned as I got in line for my meal.

Inside the mess hall, Naseeb stood rigidly next to the door. He watched over the food. This was his penalty for losing track of the rice and rifles we'd found with Gazan's fighters. The total punishment was nearly six hours standing each day. On his right side, he also wore a swollen and bluish jaw, the result of a separate and more private conversation with Commander Sabir.

As I passed through the breakfast line, I nodded to Naseeb. Despite his burdens, he offered me a broad grin that strained his tender jaw and caused a dribble to leak from the right side of his mouth. He winced and dabbed his mouth with a paper napkin. He smiled at me again and winced again. He learned slowly and suffered for it.

I took my time, and ate a tray of naan and a korma of leeks and potatoes. Then I wandered to the motor pool. Three days patrolling through the rugged mountains had pummelled our trucks, taking its toll. Since our return the entire Special Lashkar had spent long hours replacing tyres, brake pads, and even a couple blown transmissions.

When I arrived, Mortaza, Tawas, and Yar were already pulling one of our dented rims out of an otherwise good tyre. With a grunt, Mortaza slammed a jack into the space between the rubber and the metal. He stood and said: Aziz, very kind of you to join us.

I've saved you a special job, added Yar. You get to drain and replace our oil.

This was a miserable task and likely to give me a hot oil bath when I pulled the plug from the pan beneath our HiLux. I lay on my back and walked my shoulders under the chassis. Above me the chatter continued.

Whose truck is that parked next to the American's? asked Tawas.

Atal's, answered Mortaza. The man with the large house in Gomal.

Beneath our HiLux, I slowly untwisted the warm plug and shouted up to my friends: I can't see what good comes from Atal meeting with the American.

None, replied Mortaza. Issaq says the American pays him well for information. Do you think this is true?

It must be, I said. How else can you explain his expensive home or important business the morning of the shura?

Yar kicked my feet, which stuck out from beneath the chassis and flopped open at the ankles. What is any of that to any of you? he asked. Are your stomachs full? Do you have a warm place to sleep? And Aziz, is your brother treated in the hospital? With all this cared for, what the American or Atal does is no matter for us – it is not even a matter for Commander Sabir.

Our talk ended and we continued to work.

A proverb I learned in the madrassa reads: *When the friendless man passes beyond the deep place, what is his fear?* Yar had passed *the deep place* long ago. He'd left his questions and doubts there, and wouldn't abide any of ours.

We turned wrenches until our shadows were made long by the late-afternoon sun. All right, that's enough, called Yar, and we began to put our tools away. Then he grabbed me. Not quite, Aziz, he said. You were late, you clean up. We'll see you at dinner.

Mortaza and Tawas laughed as they threw their wrenches, wire brushes, and paper towels at my feet. I gathered the tools and clutched them to my chest. As I did, I saw Atal. He strolled across the motor pool, his head raised in friendly contempt of the soldiers and military equipment around him. While he walked, he stroked the running end of a clean white turban. His expression was all confidence. Trailing behind him was the girl Fareeda and the spingari Haji Jan. Fareeda's hijab was pulled tightly against her cheeks. I could see none of her black hair and her expression was clamped with pain. She followed arm in arm with Haji Jan, whose legs were bowed as wishbones. He waddled and picked at the earth in front of him with a cane that looked to be no more than a piece of root cleaved from a pine. As the two walked I couldn't tell who was helping the other along.

I stood in front of their HiLux, frozen, holding my tools. Seeing the three of them felt like an indecency, but why I couldn't say. I watched their approach, and as I did, Atal's perfume spiked the air.

Ah, salaam alaikum It is Aziz, yes? asked Atal.

I nodded.

Fareeda, he called back to the girl, you remember our friend.

She glanced towards me, her eyes lifting through a grimace.

Poor child, said Atal. I've come to get medicine for her condition. Her pain is often very bad.

It will ease soon, she said, and I saw the bottle of pills in her hand.

Haji Jan spoke to Atal, but loud enough for me to hear: If it means we avoid this place, she is better off with the old remedy.

He spat a copper jet of tobacco juice through two missing teeth.

Atal placed his hand on my shoulder. And how have you been? he asked. I understand Sabir's shura did not go well. I am sorry for that.

Before I could answer, Haji Jan planted his cane between my feet. He wagged his finger in my face and said: That dog Sabir and great men like him cause all the suffering in this world with their ideas.

I'm just a soldier, I answered.

I turned away and put some tools into a bin. Atal kissed his teeth at Haji Jan, who stepped back from me. Come, Atal said to us both, this is not the way to speak. A soldier wishes for peace more than any. But Aziz, you should know it has gotten very bad now. It is not even safe for me to leave Fareeda alone.

None are safe in the village now, said Haji Jan. Not me, not Atal, and most certainly not the girl.

I am in pain, not helpless, said Fareeda. Her breath strained against her voice.

Haji Jan shook his head with contempt for us all. Atal took Fareeda's good hand in his, and kissed it. Always a brave girl, he said. She looked at me and her eyes were black on black, swallowed by her pupils, and I thought of her rolling the ball of opium in her fingers and the contrast of her white eyes and black pupils now gripped me just as when I'd seen her robes lifted, and the contrast there, between her soft naked skin and the hard flesh of her deformity. Again I wanted her in a very savage way. I think she knew it because she wrapped her good arm around her uncle's. But she wasn't afraid. She held him as if she'd started to say goodbye.

Atal laughed a little as she clasped onto him. Come, dear, enough of that, he said. We must get on our way. Then he turned to me and said: I hope you'll finish those repairs so you can visit us again. He offered his hand in friendship. I raised my grease-stained palms to the sky as if in prayer and was glad for an excuse to avoid his manicured grip. Ah, I see, he said, well, all the best to you, Aziz.

He climbed into the driver's side of his HiLux and Fareeda climbed in on the far side. I ran around and shut the door behind her. As I did, I brushed against her dead arm and felt its hard ridges underneath her shawl. She took no note of it. She couldn't feel it and I stole this touch from her.

They sped out of the motor pool in a race with the late-afternoon sun. It was no longer safe to be on the north road at night.

*

I finished putting our tools in the large plywood bins and crossed the firebase towards the barracks. When I arrived, it was empty. Everyone was at dinner. There were no plans for work that night, so I took my time cleaning up. When I went into the shower, I scrubbed my hands until the rims of my fingernails frayed beneath the hot water. Despite my scrubbing, grease still stained my steamed palms a faded black. I put on a fresh uniform and went to the mess hall. Walking alone under a shroud of night was a pleasure that surpassed a good meal.

I took the long route so I might bump into Commander Sabir. I was anxious to hear when Taqbir would visit and perhaps bring some news of Ali. In the months since winter I hoped some of Ali's strength had returned, that the hardships I endured allowed his suffering to ease in the hospital. I was also anxious to learn when we'd next travel to Gomal so I might see Fareeda again. It'd been some weeks since our last trip. Although my days were filled with soldier's work, my thoughts never wandered far from my brother, or from her. When I thought of them,

I thought of their suffering and felt a desperate need to save them. This became very tiring, and loving them was difficult, but then I wondered if it was possible to love something you weren't trying to save.

I crossed the helicopter landing zone and walked by the HESCO-walled barracks we stayed in as recruits. Our ranks wouldn't be added to until winter. There was no time in the fighting season to train new soldiers. Naseeb now used the old barracks as a storage locker. A resupply flight had arrived while we were on patrol and pallets of rice, ammunition, and gasoline sat in the open. The cargo hadn't made it into storage. It remained untouched by the overworked and tortured Naseeb, but with such sloppy accounting, it seemed little wonder our supplies had fallen into Gazan's hands. It would be nothing to hide a couple bags of rice or a crate of ammunition in one of the binjos or trucks that passed out our front gate on business each day.

At the far corner of the firebase, Mr Jack had moved his truck from the motor pool and parked it next to the shack where he held his meetings. The moon reflected off the black HiLux, and inside the shack, Mr Jack paced, his shadow crossing the lit doorway. The idea of the sandy-haired American in that room, scheming after his meeting with Atal, exhausted me.

I entered the wide double doors of the mess hall and squinted against the glare inside. Naseeb still stood by the entrance. I got into line next to him. Most of the other soldiers had finished eating. They sat full and in a stupor on row after row of benches. The cooks spooned out my portion of greasy rice and sinewy beef and handed me an orange Fanta. I would've preferred to sit by myself, but Yar waved me over to where the rest of the squad took its meal.

I joined them, but leaned into my food to avoid conversation and to continue my solitude and rest. Although not part of the Tomahawks, Qiam sat with us. Tawas had his arm draped over his brother's shoulder. They exchanged rumours of the operations to come.

Batoor has told the Comanches that we'll avoid Gomal for a time, whispered Qiam. He says we'll let the villagers see how they enjoy Gazan's protection.

What will we do instead of building the outpost? asked Mortaza.

Batoor says we'll set up checkpoints along the north road and starve the villagers to their senses, said Qiam. Then we'll have our outpost.

Yar kissed his teeth and spoke: We will do the checkpoints. This I've heard, but not to starve innocents. Through the checkpoints, we'll find who's been smuggling our supplies to Gazan.

Everyone nodded at this idea.

Maybe Atal was here today to discuss the checkpoints, I said.

Yar fixed his gaze on me.

Atal is no concern of ours, he replied. Some things are not for knowing and those who try become fools. Everyone nodded, not necessarily in agreement, but in acknowledgement of Yar's authority. He added: Atal is a dog, and Mr Jack is his handler. You only have to tug his collar to make him look the right way.

Yar rubbed together the three fingers of his cleft rooster hand, suggesting Atal's financial itch. If it was money Atal wanted, it made sense he sold information to Mr Jack. He had the money. Mr Jack funded the Special Lashkar, too, and by that measure also owned us. As we ate our food paid for by the Americans, none of us seemed that different from Atal. And the suspicion we had for him, or the loyalty we had for each other, or the hatred we had for Gazan, all of it seemed of much less concern than the meal in front of us, and tomorrow's.

The group would sit in the mess hall and idly talk until sleep overcame them. Then they'd stagger back to the barracks. I excused myself and took my tray and dishes to the kitchen window where Naseeb now worked in a grease-stained apron behind a sink. I handed him the scraps of my meal and thanked him.

You are quite welcome, he said.

You have to do all the clean-up? I asked. This is a tough punishment.

It is not mine to question, he replied.

It is a dangerous thing Gazan's men have done, turning our supplies and guns against us, I said.

It is just the way of it, Naseeb answered. We take from them. They take from us.

This way has not worked out well for you, I told him.

Yes, yes, but if I was not here, things would be worse for me, he replied. Just as it is with you.

Yes, I agreed quietly.

Naseeb again hunched over a tall stack of plates and scrubbed. Each stroke seemed to redden his eyes and pull the colour from his fat face. The other cooks sat against the sinks and stoves, gossiping.

★

I stepped outside and sat atop a wooden picnic table that ran along the mess hall's back wall. The night was cold, but I paid it no mind. I wanted to be alone and still. I put my feet on the bench and leaned into my legs to warm my body. With my feet off the earth, the cold couldn't seep up through my boots. I buried my hands deep into my pockets and stared at a milky smudge across the night sky. I thought of my brother, far away and in the hospital, lying on his back, at the mercy of Taqbir and the supervisor with his fat paunch and sweaty bald head. The idea unnerved me, but, just like Atal, the supervisor was motivated by money, and that was a plain motivation, simple and, in its simplicity, reliable.

I also fought for money, so if men like Atal were corrupt, then so was I. As long as I stayed a soldier and my pay went to the hospital, my brother would be cared for. My war was as simple and honest as that. There was no cause in it except the cause of survival. Had I killed for money? Perhaps. Perhaps it was a round from my machine gun that had killed the man on the ridge a few days ago. I had no feud with him. If I killed him I did it for money. Atal sold information to Mr Jack for money, too, the money to care for Fareeda. What could be corrupt in that? Yet that money also paid for his large house, generator, and HiLux. Still, the truly corrupt have unreliable motivations, and money is one of the most reliable.

My eyes adjusted in the night. Slowly the outline of the motor pool, the barracks, and Commander Sabir's quarters revealed themselves. A trickle of soldiers left the mess hall. None of them noticed me sitting on the picnic table. Their eyes hadn't adjusted to the darkness, and they stumbled towards their beds.

Commander Sabir's door flew open. From it, warm tobacco smoke rose into the cold night. The squad leaders, Issaq and Batoor, emerged with faces so flushed they appeared swollen. They talked in loud drunken booms. Commander Sabir stepped between them and yawned into the sky with a silent roar. He pulled a pack of Marlboro Reds from his shoulder pocket and lit one between his teeth.

Issaq spoke, his voice flat: Give us a week before the checkpoints.

Despite all their carrying on, the three were in a negotiation.

Two days, said Commander Sabir.

But the trucks! added Issaq, growing angry.

Batoor placed a hand on Issaq's shoulder. It is enough time, he said.

Two days, repeated Commander Sabir.

Issaq ran his fingers through his hair, dyed red with henna. He nodded his head. Yes, it is enough.

Mr Jack wandered across the firebase. In the night he went unnoticed by Commander Sabir and the squad leaders. He didn't wear his sunglasses and I strained to make out his eyes, but couldn't. I wished to see the blueness I'd imagined. His steps were heavy and his full face hinted at a life unconcerned by hunger. In one hand Mr Jack carried a large dark bottle by the neck, in the other he carried a brown paper sack.

He approached slowly. When he was almost on top of the doorway, Commander Sabir saw him. Batoor and Issaq broke their conversation in mid-sentence and stumbled back to the barracks. I sat frozen on the picnic table, closed up into my body, praying I wouldn't be seen. Mr Jack held out the bottle. Maakhaam pa kheyr, Commandance Sabir, he said.

Good evening to you, too, answered Commander Sabir. So you've finally decided to come see me.

Relax, I thought we could have a drink, said Mr Jack.

Each time you bring that fool Atal to my firebase, it is an insult, snapped Commander Sabir. And now you wish us to drink as friends?

Your firebase? answered Mr Jack. I pay the bills, Sabir, and have since James fought Hafez from here. How was your operation in Gomal? Inshallah, you'll have a good fighting season.

Inshallah? Fuck you and your inshallah, said Commander Sabir. Your work with Atal does not help my operations.

Mr Jack held his index finger in Commander Sabir's face. I work with who I want, when I want. Don't forget that, he said, and continued slowly from memory: Khpal kaar saray kaar lara. Let each man turn his mind to his own concerns.

Commander Sabir kissed his teeth. Izzat kawa izzat ba dey kegi. He who respects is respected, he said, shaking his head. He put his cigarette out on the bottom of his boot and flicked the butt over Mr Jack's shoulder. He continued: Atal is not one to be involved with. When you Americans are deceived, killed in a green on blue by the very soldiers you trained, or something less, always it is done by those Afghans whose business it is to play each side against the other. Atal is one of those.

It's a business you seem to understand very well, replied Mr Jack. Is my work with him going to be a problem?

Then, in the light of the doorway, I glimpsed Mr Jack's eyes. They were faded as if the dust, the mountains, and the war had taken the blue out of them. These elements put the colour into our eyes, but seemed to take the colour from his. Commander Sabir looked at these eyes for a long moment and then spoke: No, no problem, boss.

Okay, said Mr Jack, nodding. Now, let's have a drink.

He held out the bottle of whisky and offered it, but Commander Sabir waved it away. He didn't want anything from Mr Jack, at least not right now.

Fine, Sabir, said Mr Jack. He reached into the brown paper sack he carried. From it he pulled a plastic can of fish food. But you'll need this for Omar, he added.

Commander Sabir's pet goldfish, Omar, had been a gift from Mr Jack some years before. As it was with all his gifts, this one had been given with some design to it. I later learned from Naseeb that Mr Jack thought a companion might soothe some of Commander Sabir's darker impulses, but if it had, none of us could tell. Omar always had a look of menace about him. He was missing an eye. In its place was a smooth and empty socket. That look of menace had reminded Commander Sabir of the one-eyed mullah, Mohammed Omar, the exiled leader of the Taliban. The Americans had been lucklessly chasing him for years, while Commander Sabir's Omar swam circles in his glass bowl.

Commander Sabir snatched the can of fish food from Mr Jack and opened it. He considered the smell, dipping his nose just above the flakes of freeze-dried larva, insect, and earthworm. With appreciation, he nodded to Mr Jack, not only for the food, it seemed, but also for its freshness. Taking Omar's food, but nothing else, Commander Sabir returned to his quarters, shutting the door behind him.

Mr Jack stood alone with his bottle in the night. He turned around and flipped it in the air, catching it by the neck. Then he stumbled through the darkness to his one-room shack. As soon as he was out of sight, I ran back to the barracks.

*

The next morning, I walked across the firebase to go to the bathroom. The stoves in every building poured woodsmoke into the cold dawn air, but none came from Mr Jack's shack. His black HiLux was gone.

THE RUMOURS AT THE MESS HALL proved true. The next morning Commander Sabir ordered the first checkpoints set up. While Gazan's men operated freely around Gomal and the surrounding mountains, we settled into our positions, cutting the village off from the world outside. Each day some of us would block the north road with sandbags and razor wire and others would fan out and hide among the rocks and the pines. Here we'd wait in ambush for anyone who'd sneak through the tangle of smugglers' paths that crossed the peaks and ridges.

One day, several weeks into these operations, I was standing near such a path, halfway between our firebase and Gomal. I leaned my rifle against the trunk of a pine and crouched low. It was my turn to watch for traffic. Behind me stretched a shale ridgeline. On its other side, Yar, Tawas, and Mortaza slept in our HiLux. We'd driven all night to get here and now the early-morning sun beat back the cold shadow. As day came, the mountains were pleasant and warm around me. I pulled a piece of stale naan and a packet of honey from my cargo pocket. The naan was frozen and the honey like plaster paste. Before I could finish smearing it, the hollow rumble of an engine echoed down the mountain's walls. Fear clutched my stomach. No one of honest motive travelled these narrow smugglers' paths. I dropped my food on the ground and went for my rifle and the trail below. Around a bend in the mountain, a swirl of dust sprouted. I saw a man on a motorbike, sputtering towards me. The sides of his tyres clung to the steep ridgeline.

Stop where you are! I shouted down the trail and levelled the sights of my rifle on him, unsure if I'd actually shoot. The man navigated the dangerous route with complete focus. His eyes fixed just in front of his handlebars.

He didn't stop.

His motorbike bounced and slid on the loose rock.

I called out again.

He seemed not to hear me over the noise of his engine and wouldn't stop.

And as he drew closer, his features came into focus. He was slim and young, his turban black and full. His beard was black too and hung down to his chest. Lashed above the rear tyre was a wide crate. The crate was a little longer than my rifle. It made his efforts to stay balanced all the more difficult.

He was nearly on me now, but before I could shout another warning, a shot from above hit between us. I glanced up. Yar stood on the crest, framed against the sky, sighting along his rifle. The driver looked up and saw me planted in front of him. He jerked his handlebars, hard. He toppled over them and tumbled into the shale and down the side of the ridge.

As the man fell, he did nothing to save his motorbike. Instead he dove after the crate, which had sprung loose. I walked down the path, rifle on my shoulder, eyes running the barrel, until I towered over him. He paid me no notice, but in a panic dug his sandalled heels into the rock, kicking and clawing as he heaved the crate up to the trail. The crash had knocked his turban off.

His scraped face seeped blood. He didn't notice any of this or me. Only the crate.

I stood over him and softly said: Stop or I'll shoot. At this, the driver sat down, looked up at me, and spat on the ground.

If you are a man of God, help me, please, he said. His eyes turned back to the crate. It was panelled in wood except for a pane of glass at the end. This window was intact but cracked. Inside was a small grey face garlanded in sage, thistle, and tulips. The driver's eyes shone clear with a desperate purpose. I slung my rifle across my back and picked up one end of the coffin. The driver picked up the other and we heaved it to the trail.

Yar, Tawas, and Mortaza came down the ridge towards us, their rifles slung over their shoulders. They were relaxed. What is this fool doing? called out Yar.

He needs help! I yelled back.

He's lucky we don't take him in, said Yar.

Lend a hand! I shouted.

Yar frowned and his forehead wrinkled in thought. He looked at Mortaza and Tawas and nodded towards the motorbike, which had settled halfway down the ridge. The two climbed across the loose rock on hands and knees to recover it. Yar shuffled farther down the path. With the barrel of his rifle, he motioned for the driver to stand and walk away from the coffin.

Aziz, search him, said Yar.

He is no threat, I replied.

Yar's eyes opened wide, angry.

I leaned over the man and patted down his wiry frame. Each time I touched him, the skin on his bones shifted loosely. He was ashamed to be handled like a criminal and I was ashamed to handle him as such. Neither of us could look at the other.

Finished, I held up my hands. He has nothing, I said.

Under his beard, insisted Yar.

I stood chest to chest with the man. He raised his chin and looked down his nose at me. I hung my head and reached towards his neck. I touched him lightly across it and stepped away.

Yar approached us. He glanced at the crate. What is this? he asked.

I didn't answer, but allowed him to find the small dead face. The boy's skin was smooth, almost fresh, but it lacked the fullness of youth. Where his cheeks should have been plump, the fat had melted away and they were yellowed and lean as a man's. And the loss was all in the face. What he would've grown to be in ten or fifteen years was now right there, looking back, and I think even the coldest of us, even Yar, who fought against Hafez and the Haqqanis before there was a Gazan and the Taliban, and whose own story of misery, like mine and Ali's, was so buried in him that I knew I'd never hear it, even he could see that loss. And even he could respect it.

What happened? asked Yar.

The driver's eyes twitched between his feet and the coffin. He couldn't look at the boy for too long and quickly he spoke the words: He's dead.

Yes, I see that, replied Yar in a tone approaching tenderness. How did he die?

The man stood and fixed us in his gaze. His chest expanded and seemed to grow inches as he breathed hate into his lungs. My nephew, he said, was outside another village stealing food – pine nuts. The men there shot him as a thief, and left him on the hillside among the trees.

You will take badal against those who did this? Yar asked the man.

He nodded.

So bury your nephew and fight alongside us, Yar said. If Gazan is pushed out of Gomal, the suffering there ends.

He shook his head. What badal is there in that? he asked.

We will make Gazan and his men bleed, said Yar. There is your badal.

The man's next words came out hateful and quick: If he bleeds or if you bleed, it is of no difference to me.

The man shouldered past us to where Tawas and Mortaza had heaved his motorbike back to the trail. He reached into the dirt and coiled a piece of rope over his elbow and thumb. With the rope, he lashed the coffin above his back tyre.

We've helped you, I said. To say you'd see us bleed is unjust.

The man dropped his coil of rope. He stared at the ground. Then he looked up at us. His eyes were hard and smooth, but shaking. Unjust? he said. You knocked me off this trail, which I drive because your feud with Gazan blocks the north road. My nephew is dead because you starve my village. Now I will bury him far from your fighting. Badal is all I have left and my badal is to deny myself to you, to Gazan, or to any other who speaks of blood.

The driver went back to his lashing. Then, finished, he straddled his motorbike, kick-started it, and sputtered past us down the trail.

*

We watched the driver and his coffin disappear where the mountains became like a braid in the north. Tawas replaced me on the trail and the rest of us walked back over the ridge and hid beneath the crest where boulders scooped shade from the sun. Here we struggled to sit comfortably along a field of shale and every so often stones shifted underfoot and a small rockslide crashed down the mountain's front. Each time this happened, Yar gazed meanly at us. The day wore on with sitting, rockslides, and trail duty.

We longed for nightfall and our return to the firebase. Then, late in the afternoon, another dust cloud climbed from the distance. Yar looked towards Mortaza and me with a cold stare that demanded we remain still. The cloud wove through the mountain's fingers, coming ever closer. On the trail Tawas stood stupid and unmovable, chewing his bubblegum with the blank look of a cow chewing its cud.

A pair of motorbikes appeared. Each carried two men. The first driver saw Tawas straight away and broke hard, nearly toppling end over end. The second driver rocked back and forth, trying to see up the trail and cursing the front two for stopping. This continued long enough for me to push up on the balls of my feet so I might gain a better view. As I did this, I saw one of the men from the second motorbike run to the first. Then the ground beneath my high crouch gave out, crumbling shale stones from the mountainside. Seeing this, the four men dropped their motorbikes. In a panic they ran in four different directions. Yar fired steadily from his rifle into the air. The men froze.

Lie down! shouted Yar and his voice echoed across the ridge as though it were that of God, and the men responded as such, bowing to the ground and searching for the voice.

Shall we interrogate our prisoners? Yar asked us through a smile.

We jogged down the side of the mountain towards the men. One at a time Yar grabbed them by the backs of their shirts and lined them up along the trail. He pushed them down, hard, so they squatted awkwardly on their haunches. Mortaza helped. The two pulled flex-cuffs tight against the men's wrists and the plastic cut into their skin. Our prisoners craned their necks, twitching like birds that clutch the same limb, trying to glimpse us.

Tawas ran up the trail. Yar pointed at him and cried out: You and Aziz check their things.

Their motorbikes lay in the road like a pair of sunning dogs. We rifled through the small bundles lashed on the back. The men didn't have much with them – a few heavy wool blankets, three large bottles of orange Fanta, and a couple plastic shopping bags filled with stale naan and dried apricots. Tawas tucked his bubblegum behind his ear and drank from one of the bottles of orange Fanta. He offered me a sip, but I refused. I didn't want to steal from these men.

There were no weapons, but this didn't mean the men weren't Gazan's fighters. All four were military age, and fighters often travelled from place to place unarmed in case of checkpoints such as ours.

Yar stood over the men as I came up behind him. They have nothing but bedding and some food, I whispered in his ear. He shrugged and gave my report as much weight as if I'd told him what I'd had for breakfast.

What do you all know of Gazan? The question was met with silence and downcast eyes. Yar nudged one of the men in the back with his boot. The man, who was perched awkwardly on his haunches, couldn't stop himself from slowly toppling face-first to the ground. Yar leaned down and placed his eyes level with the man's. He growled: You expect me to believe none of you know who Gazan is?!

The man lay with his cheek in the dirt and his hands bound behind him. His breaths turned to grunts as he used his neck and shoulders to lever himself upright. Of course I've heard of Gazan, he said, but I don't know him.

Yar snorted back. He shot a wad of spit on the ground and kicked the wet gob into the man's face. Watching, I winced. These men had no weapons and as far as we could prove had done nothing. Their presence on the trail was difficult to explain, but this seemed too much.

Our prisoners sat on their haunches stupid with fear, fear of Yar, and, I realised, fear of me. Their limbs were folded at tight angles but none of them had enough meat on his body to strain against the awkward position. Yar walked between the four bundles of joints, flesh, and dirty clothes and spat another question: Where are you travelling from?

None replied. They tried to make themselves inconspicuous, each holding on to the three-in-four chance that they would avoid Yar's next round of interrogation. Yar took his time as he selected his victim. He enjoyed torturing the men with his choice. He casually crouched alongside one of the prisoners, who had a smooth face. There was the loud crack of flesh against flesh as Yar slapped the man across the cheek with the three callused talons of his mangled hand. Again he spat his question in a hot whisper: I asked, where are you travelling from?

The smooth-faced man whimpered against the strike, but managed to keep his footing. His eyes bulged wide, the whites netted in a red web of veins. A violet thistle in the lapel of his vest stood defiantly against Yar and he sniffed against the pain. We are travelling musicians looking for work, he said.

Yar canted his head to the side, puzzled.

Behind Yar, Tawas laughed and orange Fanta bubbled up through his nose. He wiped his chin and the smooth-faced man grinned at him. Yar looked back and canted his head to the other side. He also grinned and then struck the smooth-faced man with the full and closed fist of his good hand. Yar's blow pulled the man's feet from under him and he hung in the air for a noticeable moment before he landed on his side. At this, the other three prisoners took a sharp breath. So too did Tawas.

I took a full step away from Yar.

He pulled another prisoner up by his bound wrists. The man was ugly with a flat nose, large ears, and the wide Mongol face of a Hazara. He stood eye to eye and chest to chest with Yar, but he trembled and looked very small. Yar enjoyed his trembling and again snorted, his nostrils flaring. If a flat-faced chungayz such as you is a musician, he said, where is your instrument? Before the ugly man could answer, Yar pushed him backward. He lost his balance and toppled to his side next to the smooth-faced man. The ugly one and his friend slowly rose to their feet. The smooth-faced man's thistle had been crushed and it wilted from his lapel, absurdly. The two presented themselves before Yar, their clothes filthy and hair now matted with fine dust. Yar leaned back and laughed. I thought he laughed at their sorry appearance, but soon I knew he laughed at his power over them.

The scene was shameful. These men had no nang. They took Yar's beatings without fighting back. But Yar had no shame in delivering his blows. One of the men on the end who had escaped Yar whimpered: We find instruments where we go. We don't have the money for our own.

The snivelled response was too much for Mortaza. Any more of you dogs open your mouths and we'll break your skulls, he sneered.

Yar nodded his approval. I can't stand to look at these dar-wankee, pussies, he said and flicked his wrist for Mortaza and me to take them away. We heaved the four men to their feet and pushed them up the shale slope. Our HiLux was parked in the ravine on the opposite side. Mortaza and I marched our silent group in a single file. No one spoke. The shame of being beaten like an animal, the shame of watching a friend suffer, the shame of abusing helpless men. Silence brought us shame and the shame brought us to silence.

Tawas stayed back with Yar and they rolled hand grenades under the motorbikes. Two low thumps, like cans of soda being crushed, echoed down the ravine. The four men kept their eyes on the loose shale in front of them as they listened to their possessions being destroyed.

Why did the men have no instruments? I took comfort in this and imagined Gazan and his fighters searching for their missing comrades and finding only two destroyed motorbikes. What other business could these men have had on the trail? Whatever sympathy they wanted us to feel for them was a deceit. If we let them prey on our sympathies, later they would find us, or our comrades, and we would be the victims as their real nature was known. I made a loop of this in my mind, layering it into the truth I thought it should be. And maybe it was.

Our HiLux sat in the ravine, dented and painted grey as the mountain. Mortaza and I loaded our prisoners in its bed. A chill grew in the air and announced the night before the sunset. For them, the ride in the cold would be an added brutality. They wore nothing but their thin shirts. None of us wanted to sit with them on the long journey back to Shkin.

Aziz, stay in the bed, Yar told me. Mortaza, you drive for a bit.

But I can drive, I protested.

Yes, but you're better on the gun, said Yar, opening the door to the cab.

What about Tawas? I asked.

Yar looked at him, bubblegum tucked behind his ear, still guzzling orange Fanta, which dribbled down the front of his shirt. Yar shook his head. Yes, it's best that you be on the gun, he said.

Mortaza gave me a cruel smile.

Pa kona da keegda, shove it in your ass, I told him and spat on the ground.

I slid the water, ammunition, and other supplies around in back to make myself a comfortable seat, then I crammed a prisoner into each corner, an inconvenient cargo. I climbed onto my perch, our HiLux's engine turned over, and we crept along the soft pebbles of the ravine. I leaned against the cab and rested my palm on the machine gun's buttstock. Lazily it swung from side to side. A large crate of ammunition stuck awkwardly out from the front right corner of the bed. Here the smooth-faced man sat. His arms were jammed behind his back. Each time we hit a bump, the crate crushed his fingers. He winced, but made no noise for fear of another beating. I pulled a knife from my belt and reached behind him. Seeing the blade, he flinched, but when I cut his flex-cuffs loose and his hands sprang free, he offered me a full white grin that could be seen even in the fading light. I returned my hand to the machine gun's buttstock and allowed our truck to sway me back and forth like an infant. The smooth-faced man fixed the thistle in his lapel and tapped out a beat against the aluminium bed. The other man, the ugly one, hummed softly and their song travelled along the mountains and back to our firebase.

OUR PATROL ARRIVED at the firebase in time for a half night's sleep. Shortly before we entered the front gate, I tightened a fresh set of flex-cuffs on the smooth-faced prisoner. As I did, he looked up at me and seemed more upset than if I had left his hands bound for the whole ride back. And what thanks was that? I became sick of staring at him and his three friends and couldn't care less whether they were four Taliban or four musicians. We delivered them into a one-room hut with a heavy padlock, their home until Commander Sabir decided what he wanted done with them. As for me, I reminded myself I was a soldier and forgot them. And several nights later, when an unscheduled helicopter landed at the firebase, and then afterwards, when the mud hut was empty, I reminded myself again.

None of us came to the Special Lashkar to sit on checkpoints. We came for badal against Gazan. We began to think Commander Sabir's outpost would prevent that. For him nothing was more important than the outpost. From it, he could extend his control over a large swath of the border, regulating anything and anyone who wished to cross. He'd also pledged to hunt down Gazan from here. But if we killed Gazan, the villagers would never let us maintain the outpost. We would've removed the threat that gave us power over them. Destroying Gazan and his fighters would never be a good option for Commander Sabir. He needed them.

The spingaris resisted the outpost, but we kept pressure on them through our checkpoints and by allowing Gazan's mortar attacks into Gomal. There things had become so bad that it was rumoured some of the spingaris had changed their minds about our proposal. When enough of them did, Commander Sabir would get his outpost.

He would prosper in it. Not only would he control the border, but he'd receive kickbacks from his friends in Orgun and Kabul who would bid on the contracts to build the outpost. To man it, the Americans would surely add more soldiers to our payroll, money that Commander Sabir pilfered. None of this could happen without Gazan.

In Pashto, Commander Sabir's type of war is called ghabban: this is when someone demands money for protection against a threat they create. For this type of war, the Americans don't have a word. The only one that comes near is *racket*. Our war was a racket.

I know that now.

The next morning at breakfast, Yar told all who would listen about our adventure at the checkpoint. He leaned over his food and said: As the two motorbikes came on Tawas, he stood frozen, his feet like roots grown into the middle of the trail.

Did he finally move? someone called out.

Yar clasped Tawas by the shoulder. This is a courageous one, he said, ignorant of fear, stupidly brave! He did not move but stood, daring Gazan's fighters to charge him, and instead they skidded off the trail.

Did they run? asked someone else.

I shot a single burst, said Yar, and all four froze like little boys when their fathers call. Yar jumped on his seat, unslung his Kalashnikov, and put it between his legs. Thrusting with his hips, he shouted: But now I was their father!

Hoots and laughter filled the mess hall. From the far corner Commander Sabir watched. His split lip pulled over his bottom teeth, unrolling into an ugly smile. He looked down at his food.

I finished breakfast and rushed to the motor pool. I hoped to see Mr Jack's black HiLux or Atal's white one parked among ours. Imperfect and secretive as they were, these two served as my only beacons to that life which existed outside Commander Sabir's authority. On this hilltop the values of his universe were total and my own threatened to be lost in them. Years ago, up on the roof of our house, Ali once taught me the trick our father used whenever he got lost in the mountains. Ali took out a compass and showed me how to get a reading from two points and to draw those lines on a map. He explained how I could always be found where the lines crossed. For his example, he used the bazaar in Sperkai and the beacon on the radio tower, the one whose red light filled my father's ruby. When he drew the lines, they met right over us.

But that morning, in those mountains, I could see no farther than our beat-up truck, which we'd parked in the centre of the motor pool's gravel lot. I pulled my tools from a plywood bin and worked beneath it. I couldn't say what I worked on that day or the next, for that matter. Life at the firebase had become an endless repetition of vehicle checkpoints and maintenance routines.

Just like all of us, Issaq hoped to go on the offensive. At least twice a week he took our squad to a compound of abandoned mud huts by the range. Here we practised raids. The huts' thatched roofs had collapsed long ago and Issaq scrambled up a three-rung ladder to stand atop their bare walls. He watched as each of his teams worked through the mechanics of clearing a compound. We flooded the rooms, screaming after invisible enemies and each other. Issaq looked down at us shouting corrections: Clear your sector! Who's covering that window! Check the dead space! He kept a handful of gravel in his cargo pocket. If one of us made the wrong turn at a door or in a hall, he struck a rock off our helmet. Sometimes he missed, and rocks to the face, shoulders, or ankles were common. After each turn through the house, he leapt off the roof, corrected us all, and then set up tables and chairs as obstacles for the next run. This added to the difficulty and we rushed through the house again, throwing anything in our path across the room. Training eased our impatience for action, for a while.

*

The weather warmed and the sky was clear for days at a time. The resupply helicopters swarmed into Shkin and we spent long hours on the gravel landing zone, crawling over pallets and running up and down the helicopters' ramps while Naseeb shouted confused directions and the rotors swept our faces with hot dust. The flights brought in food and ammunition, fresh vegetables and fruit, and pieces of the world beyond our firebase, including the occasional visitor.

Early on a Friday morning, I sat at a picnic table outside the mess hall and ate from a small bag of oranges flown in the night before. The previous afternoon we'd returned from checkpoint duty and had been given this day off. As I lazed, Taqbir walked past. I hadn't seen him in months. He strolled by casually, heading to breakfast. His uniform rested crisply on his shoulders and his powerful torso filled it out with well-fed muscles. He looked no different from when I'd met him last winter, but I saw him differently.

Taqbir! I cried.

He continued to walk. I ran up alongside him and grabbed his elbow. He gazed down his hawkish face at me, pulled his arm away, and looked at his sleeve, concerned perhaps that my hands had stained his fresh uniform.

It is Aziz, yes? he asked.

Yes! I said, my voice brimming with joy. How is my brother?

Yes, Aziz, he said, slowing his speech as if he were thinking of something else. Of course, and your brother . . .

Ali, I said, too desperate to consider Taqbir had forgotten him.

Yes, Ali, said Taqbir. He stopped and pulled a stuffed envelope from his cargo pocket. He sifted through its many scraps of paper. He then pulled out a dog-eared photo, examined it quickly, and held it to his chest. Your brother is the one who lost a leg and has . . . other injuries, he replied, both asking and telling me this.

I stood silently and tried not to snatch the photo. Taqbir looked at me, awaiting my response. Yes, I said. He lost his leg in the bombing at the bazaar a few months ago.

Yes, Bombing at the Bazaar, said Taqbir, as if Bombing at the Bazaar were Ali's new name.

He handed me the photo. I held it close to my face and devoured it with my eyes.

He is well and asks of you often, said Taqbir, his voice flat and rehearsed. I assure him you are fine. He knows you're fighting to take badal and that you're poised to deliver a great blow against Gazan and his thugs. I pray for the day when I can give him news of your victory.

I listened, but heard very little. All I could do was stare at the photo. In it, Ali lay on a bed with a half-empty sheet covering him. The blood at his waist was gone. The joints on his withered frame poked against his hospital gown. His sunken face was unshaven and turned away from the camera. He gazed across the room as if somewhere out of the picture a ghost lingered. What was the ghost my brother stared at?

You say he is well? I asked.

He is, said Taqbir. He thinks only of you and the peace he will know when badal is taken and his nang restored. Taqbir clasped my shoulder and raised his eyebrows. He tucked the envelope full of photographs and notes back into his pocket, except for Ali's, which he offered me. When you look at that, he said, think of your brother and what you will do to those who harmed him.

Taqbir continued to the mess hall.

I sat on the picnic table holding the photo. My mind felt like an emptiness waiting to be filled. Then, very clearly, I remembered the last time I spoke to Ali. In my panic, I'd told him about algebra and how the word meant to make whole from parts. And I thought it could be like this with my brother. Maybe badal was a type of algebra. If I could stand over Ali and whisper that those who had taken everything from him now suffered as he did, maybe that could make some part of him whole, maybe that could kill the ghost. It would never be as it was before, but perhaps badal could be enough to hold us together. I tucked the photograph into my cargo pocket and returned to the barracks.

The squad lay in rows of plywood beds, enjoying the day off, sleeping and talking. At a checkpoint the morning before, Tawas had snared a magpie with a wire noose and a piece of stale naan. He'd managed to fashion a cage of sapling branches for the black-and-white bird. He hung the cage above his bed on the nail where the rest of us hung our rifles. Tawas sat on his knees. He faced the cage and pleaded with the bird: Gul, Flower, sing for me. Chi-chi-charee, chi-chi-charee.

The magpie was silent but for the flapping of its few blue tailfeathers.

Come, Gul, said Tawas, tapping at his cage. Chi-chi-charee, chi-chi-charee.

Yar kissed his teeth. Your bird's a mute, he said. Give him to me and I'll have Naseeb prepare him for dinner.

He'll sing, said Tawas. Come, Gul. Chi-chi-charee, chi-chi-charee.

Then Mortaza said, as if he knew: Tawas, the bird will only sing caw-caw-catoo, caw-caw-catoo.

But the magpie canted his head and gave Mortaza a silent look. Yar pulled a bullet out of one of his magazines. Strike at the bird's cage, he said. That's the best way to make it sing!

Yar threw the bullet at the cage. It bounced from its ribs and fell to the floor. The magpie flapped its wings, but stared back at us silently. Yar grunted. You call him Gul? he said. You should call him Puskie, Silent Fart.

We all laughed and agreed, even Tawas. We'd call the magpie Puskie.

*

As conversation fell away, I stretched out on my bed. Across from me, Tawas napped on his side. Above his head Puskie sang low: chi-chi-charee, chi-chi-charee. His song worked as a reverse alarm clock, taking me to sleep instead of waking me from it.

My legs and back loosened with the tune: chi-chi-charee, chi-chi-charee. Soon Puskie's black feathers, white body, and blue tail flashed and then fluttered across my mind: chi-chi-charee, chi-chi-charee.

I drifted.

Angry shouts came. A metal gate shook. SABIR! SABIR! These words fell on me, as quick and blurred as the bird's feathers. I couldn't tell if the sounds were pulling me into my dream or back awake.

SABIRSABIRSABIR! The name quickened, blending into itself, no longer a word but a song of absolute suffering.

All around me was shuffling.

I was awake.

Issaq rushed from our barracks. Tawas and Mortaza followed him. I rose quickly from my bed and stepped outside. The late-morning air was cool and the clouds hung grey and low. In the courtyard of the firebase, a crowd was forming. I joined them.

Across the firebase two white binjos were stuck at the entrance. The drivers leaned on their horns while a bearded man heaved up the gate's large red-and-white arm. In his eyes there was a madness. A bib of blood smeared his shirtfront, and again came his song: SABIRSABIRSABIR!

Stop! We will shoot! The guards shouted from their towers.

Commander Sabir ran from his quarters in stocking feet, crossing the courtyard. Khar, donkeys! he shouted back. No one's shooting anyone!

I walked closer. The man at the entrance was Atal. He looked savage, on edge, all reserve and elegance having slipped from his grip like a shroud held loosely to the wind.

Commander Sabir waved for the guards to come down and lift the gate. They did and the two binjos kicked up a cloud of dust, speeding into the motor pool, their open doors flapping as broken wings do. Atal was left stranded at the gate. The dust from the binjos stuck to him like batter. He stumbled slowly onto the firebase, his wild black hair caked upward and his chest thrust towards any soldier who'd approach him. Two streams branched from his eyes, rutting canals in his dirty cheeks, pouring tears into his full beard.

By now the barracks had emptied. Soldiers surrounded the pair of binjos. Make way! Make way! shouted Issaq. And he cleared a path for a medic. The driver of the second binjo opened its trunk. This made an overhang against the sun. The medic approached and stood next to the driver in the shadow beneath it. They both looked inside. The medic reached into the binjo and raised Haji Jan up in his arms, carrying him like a sleeping child. In this moment, I glimpsed the face of the ancient spingari. His skin had lost much colour, and drying blood spattered his cheeks as freckles do the cheeks of those with fair skin. He was alive, though. I could see his lips move all the while, whispering something not meant to be heard, not by me and not by the medic who carried him.

The few villagers who'd driven up from Gomal circled around Haji Jan, so too did many of us soldiers. Haji Jan quickly disappeared into the crowd. Once at the double doors of the clinic, Issaq shouted at the onlookers: Outside! Outside! And from the mass came the medic and Haji Jan. Issaq held the doors open and followed them through.

Commander Sabir returned to his quarters, where he stood in the doorway. He didn't watch the drama at the clinic. He watched Atal, who inched towards him with purpose, his pale green eyes sharp compared to his dust-covered face and blood-stained clothes. Hanging beneath Atal's beard was the opal on the chain of braided silver. He clutched the stone as he walked.

I considered Atal for a moment longer. The dust that covered him was not just from the road and the binjos, it had been made by something more destructive, something that shredded clothing, broke skin, and wove shards of concrete and glass into his hair and beard. Whatever had made the dust had also made the blood that stained his shalwar kameez. And this blood was not entirely Haji Jan's. Around the ribs the stain came up from beneath, pasting Atal's shirt to his body.

Fareeda ran out of the parked binjo to help him. Her steps were quick and short. Blood had also blotched lightly against the white linen of her hijab, so lightly it appeared pink. She tucked her head underneath Atal's arm. He leaned heavily on her left shoulder, and from her right shoulder the large deformed limb hung lifeless.

Commander Sabir spotted me watching. What's wrong with you! he shouted. Help our guests.

I ran to Atal, but after a few steps he stopped me with a raised palm. He shook his head and said: Your help is not necessary. Then he stumbled forwards as he leaned against Fareeda, who noted me with a glance.

Commander Sabir dismissed the pair's defiance with a flick of his wrist, but I walked alongside them in case I was needed. Atal continued, grunting and shuffling, his elbow covering his side. Soon he presented himself in front of Commander Sabir, wincing with pain as he stood straight.

It looks like you have some broken ribs, my friend, said Commander Sabir. We can speak once you've been seen in the clinic and checked on Haji Jan.

Atal took short and careful breaths. I can be seen later, he said. As for Haji Jan, what's best for him is for you and me to attend to our business.

Commander Sabir shrugged and waved them inside. Being the only soldier nearby, he ordered me to bring some tea, so I ran to the mess hall, crossing the open courtyard where others still crowded around the windows of the clinic. Quickly, I gathered a tray and returned to Commander Sabir's quarters. I stood in the small entryway, listening to the muffled but rising voices inside the bedroom. I knocked on the paint-chipped door. Commander Sabir pushed it open. He and Atal sat cross-legged, facing each other on a red-and-black rug of Persian design. Fareeda sat behind Atal and off to his side. Apart from the rug, the room was empty but for Commander Sabir's unmade bed with its swirl of sheets – Naseeb had put aside the complete *Masters of the Universe* set for him – and the end table by his pillow, where Omar swam circles, trapped in his bowl.

As I served tea, Commander Sabir shook his can of fish food over the bowl. Flakes of dried insect and worm parts snowed down on the water's surface and then sank beneath it. Omar paddled through this storm. He was huge, almost as big as a rat. He was all mouth and thick tail, lapping at the food. His one eye sat on the side of his black head, large as a pea. The rest of him was black too, except in direct light, where he shone gold. Atal spoke, Commander Sabir listened, but kept his eyes on the circling fish.

You and Gazan have gone too far.

Gazan has gone too far, replied Commander Sabir, tapping his fingernail against the glass bowl, slurping tea over his broken lower lip.

Don't speak to me as a fool who doesn't understand the way of things. You two are the same and have gone too far, said Atal. Against his cracked ribs, he strained to sit upright. The smell of his perfume lingered in the air, its sharpness mixing with the scents of blood and earth.

I have done nothing to harm Gomal, quite the opposite, said Commander Sabir, moving his stare from the fishbowl to Atal. I promised you an outpost to keep off Gazan's fighters. You and Haji Jan refused my generosity. This violence is the result. Are you surprised?

What if you'd built your outpost? asked Atal. Already Gazan's men mortar us relentlessly because he fears we may support you. His rounds landed on my house, MY HOUSE! And did this. He pointed to his bloodstained clothes and continued: And an honoured spingari such as Haji Jan lies bleeding in your clinic. This attack, this attack could've killed her! he said, reaching behind him and grabbing Fareeda's good arm.

Emotion choked off his words. He tilted his head back and paused to keep the tears in his full eyes from flooding down his face again. With his gaze upturned, he didn't notice that Commander Sabir fought against a desire to smile, but I did. He hadn't forgotten Haji Jan's insults at the shura. Commander Sabir turned his attention to Fareeda.

Thanks to God you were not hurt, child.

Fareeda cast her eyes towards the ground, as though staring at the disfigurement in Commander Sabir's face was too much a reminder of her own. I am fine, she answered. Thank you.

Your well-being is something we can be grateful for on such a black day, said Commander Sabir. And your arm, does it trouble you?

He moved to touch it.

Atal cuffed his wrist, pushing it away. The arm is fine, he said.

I am glad to hear that, replied Commander Sabir, and now he was smiling. The medicine you get from the American is working, then? It must be very expensive to fight such a horrible disease.

Atal stared back, his neck becoming tense, thick, and red.

It is nothing that I know this, said Commander Sabir. I work with the Americans too. The wealth you've built through them has given you a great voice with the people of Gomal. Next to Haji Jan, I think you command the most respect, or at least the most power in the shura. So explain to your village that we all must work together. You've always been practical in caring for Fareeda. Come, be practical in caring for your village.

With Fareeda, I am practical in fighting her disease, said Atal.

Yes, very practical, and she is alive.

In my village, you are the disease.

That is not the way of it, said Commander Sabir. Gazan is the disease, and with him so active, we too must be active. Then his voice turned very flat: But if nothing is done, well, I imagine you may find yourself in Haji Jan's position.

Atal became quiet, choosing his words: Do you speak a threat?

I speak only of what is obvious, said Commander Sabir. If my outpost had been built, Gazan would not have struck at Haji Jan so. But if there is no outpost, I think things will end badly for all.

You and Gazan make our homes a battlefield, said Atal with hate in his voice.

There's a war here, said Commander Sabir. You can't control that. What you can do is choose a side. To not choose is a luxury you don't have.

Tell me, how much will you make off the contracts for the outpost? asked Atal. How much more will the Americans pay you? You care nothing for my village. I choose the path that gives you nothing and ends your war.

Commander Sabir poured Atal and then Fareeda another cup of tea. He dabbed his lip and tried to smile at the girl. War's end? he asked. War only ends for those who allow others to fight for them, but there is always fighting. My brother fought Hafez and the Haqqanis. Then he was killed. Then I killed Hafez. Now there is Gazan and his Taliban. None of this can be stopped, but maybe I can take the war somewhere else, maybe to a village that isn't yours, but first the outpost. This is the way of it.

Atal sipped his tea, breathed deeply, and cringed against his breath. There is no difference between you and Gazan, he said. You offer me the same thing.

One of us is more powerful than the other, said Commander Sabir. There is your difference. Perhaps that's why you're speaking to me before Gazan and perhaps why you've spoken to Mr Jack before me. It is time to choose.

Without a knock, the door to Commander Sabir's quarters swung open. Issaq stepped into the room. His face was sweaty. Our eyes rested on him and then on his hands, which were slick with dark greasy blood. Issaq seemed to feel our gazes holding there and wiped his palms against the seat of his pants. He parted his lips as if to speak to Commander Sabir. But as he did, he caught a glimpse of Atal and Fareeda. He breathed in quickly, pulling back his words. Slowly, Issaq shook his head.

Commander Sabir looked at Atal to see if he understood.

Atal set his tea down and strained up to his feet. Thank you for your efforts, he said to Issaq. Then he spoke to Commander Sabir: Now that Haji Jan is dead, I must bury him before the sun sets. If there is nothing else, I'd like to return to my village to do this. That we can both agree is proper under God's eyes.

Of course, said Commander Sabir. I'll radio our checkpoints on the north road and tell them you're coming.

Please do, said Atal. On the way here, we were nearly shot approaching them.

You should've come in your HiLux, not the binjo, Commander Sabir said. Had they seen it was you, they would've let you pass.

Atal looked towards Fareeda.

Haji Jan and I were unconscious in the rubble, he said. She is the one who went for help. I only awoke on the drive here.

Commander Sabir nodded towards Fareeda with respect. You have Gazan to thank for this, he told Atal. It is time to choose.

I'll be on my way, he replied.

Yes. On your way, said Commander Sabir. But first let Aziz help you to the clinic.

Atal grimaced as he stepped from the room. Fareeda and I ran to his side. We held him under his elbows. He walked stiffly into a late-morning wind that blew dust across the courtyard of the firebase. I shut the door behind us, catching a glimpse of Commander Sabir. He tapped on the glass bowl with his fingernail, but Omar had lost interest in him. Instead the goldfish paddled his tail, nosing at the last few flecks of food, which had settled along a bed of bright blue, red, and green gravel.

The three of us shuffled to the clinic, where a few curious soldiers still gawked at the windows. I pushed the creaking doors open and Atal thanked me. I tried to follow him in, but he held up his hand and asked if I would wait outside with Fareeda.

I nodded and Atal passed by us.

*

She looked at me, lost. Sit here, I said, and pointed to the long single row of wood benches that rested against the clinic wall. With her one hand, she pulled her skirts flat against the back of her legs and sat. I stood over her. Her dark eyes seemed to reflect a small glimmer of sun despite the mat of clouds that covered the sky. Wisps of perfect black hair fell against her smooth forehead. Her skin was a dim ivory colour, fine and deep. She heaved her deformed arm across her lap with the opposite hand, and then spoke past me and towards the mountains: It is always this way with the dying, isn't it?

What way? I asked.

That one is killed, she said, and then something must be done. What will be done for Haji Jan? I asked.

I don't know, but something will be done, she said. Now my uncle is the most important of the spingaris. Commander Sabir will want him to support the outpost and the villagers will want badal for Haji Jan.

Maybe something should be done, I told her. Maybe Haji Jan is dead because nothing was ever done to Gazan, but you are young and a woman. This is not how you should speak.

How do I speak? she asked.

Of killing and of death, I said.

When those things are my life, I speak of my life.

I smiled. If those things are your life, then you are like a soldier.

She smiled back, but her face quickly flattened. To survive in a soldier's world, all must be like soldiers.

Yes, but to fight is what only the soldier does.

You think it is only the soldier who fights? she asked, her eyes turning to narrow slits. I fight every day to keep this from killing me. She pointed with her good arm to the bad one that lay heavily across her lap, hidden beneath the blue shawl that hung lightly atop her shoulders. She continued, her breath mixing with her words: It spreads across me and without medicine it will consume me.

What does your medicine do? I asked.

It makes it so the blood cannot clot in the arm. Her voice softened: A clot could move and stop my heart.

I felt her vulnerability, but still I continued: So the medicine is expensive?

Yes, she said, and hard to find.

And the opium? I asked.

She threw her eyes from me.

It is only for the pain, she answered. Even though it might carry me away, I have nothing else for the pain.

Then, slowly, her gaze returned to mine.

If the attack had killed my uncle, she said, it would've killed me too. When the war killed my father, I had no one to care for me, but my uncle, he saved me and still does.

I sat down next to her on the bench. He is blessed to have you, I said.

And you? she asked. Do you have someone?

I have my brother, but he is in Orgun, in the hospital.

I am sorry, she replied. Still you are blessed to have him.

Yes, I said, but it is difficult.

It is not the difficulties, but to suffer them alone.

Fareeda and I waited outside the clinic for a long time. I offered to bring her to the mess hall for lunch, but she refused. She didn't want to leave.

May I lie on the bench? she asked. I am tired.

Of course, I said.

She shut her eyes for a moment, then looked up at me, asking: You will wake me when my uncle comes?

Of course, I said again, but there wasn't enough room for me to sit and for her to lie down, so I sat in the dirt with my back against the wall of the clinic. She lay on her side and as she did, her eyes became level with mine. She seemed happy that I would sit in the dirt for her. Slowly, looking at me, she fell asleep, and I watched over her, and there was such a softness to her face that I knew she was very beautiful.

The double doors of the clinic swung open. Atal and several others from the village heaved a bundle shrouded in a white kafan on their shoulders. None of the men strained against the weight, except for Atal, who despite his broken ribs took his place among Haji Jan's pallbearers. He shuddered as he walked, but there was a great dignity to him. He had cleaned the dust from his face and wore a fresh shalwar kameez from our supply locker. Wind blew against him, pulling his shirt tight and I could see the outline of an immense bandage wrapped around his chest.

Another gust snatched the corner of the kafan and flapped up its edge to reveal the black rubber of the body bag beneath. Fareeda leapt from the bench to Atal's side. He waved her away, determined to carry Haji Jan without help. I followed, but Atal waved his hand again, releasing me from my vigil over Fareeda. The men of Gomal loaded Haji Jan's body into the back of the second binjo. Atal grabbed the car's roof as he eased himself into the passenger seat. He leaned against the headrest and his fingertips wiped the weariness from his eyes. Fareeda sat behind him. As she did, she looked out from the back seat, past the body, and caught my eye. I think she knew it was wrong to take a look in this way, but I was glad for it.

The late-afternoon sun broke through the clouds and rested its long shadows in the valleys below the mountains. The early-summer day would hold its light for a few more hours and Atal would return to his village with time to slip Haji Jan into the earth, covering him with the loose shale stones that for the spingari's entire life had crept slowly, by inches, down the mountainside towards his grave.

Across the courtyard, Commander Sabir stood in the doorway to his quarters, still in his stocking feet. He watched Atal's departure. The two binjos turned the road to dust and left the firebase, descending into a cloud they'd created. And as the red-and-white gate arm crashed down behind them, Commander Sabir looked at the ground, shook his head, and walked inside.

AFTER ATAL LEFT it was time for dinner, but I had no appetite. I returned to our barracks, where Puskie sang quietly in the corner. Mortaza leaned against his foam mattress, holding a long switch bowed under its own weight. When the bird grew silent, he snapped the switch against the cage and Puskie sang again. I walked down the barracks' empty centre aisle. Mortaza wore his uniform and a pair of unlaced white high tops with a gold stripe across the side. The shoes hung on his feet loosely, in a casual way. When he saw me, he pushed himself up on his elbows. Why aren't you at dinner? he asked.

Why aren't you? I asked him back.

Mortaza stared past me. I need a break from them, he said.

Me too, I replied and lay on my bunk, which was alongside his. Neither of us spoke. Instead we listened to Puskie's chirping. He'd start his tune low: chi-chi-charee, then a little higher: *chi-chi-charee*, and then explode, full-chested, almost hysterical: CHI-CHI-CHAREE-CHI-CHI-CHAREE! Puskie would flap his wings and thump his chest until suddenly, and just as violently, he'd begin again with a low chi-chi-charee, chi-chi-charee. Each time he went through this cycle, Mortaza and I threw one another an amused glance from across our bunks.

We saw the futility in Puskie's song. It always came to the same end.

But now and then Puskie would forget to begin and Mortaza would strike his cage with the switch, hard, to remind him of his purpose.

Puskie stalled once more. I looked at Mortaza, expecting him to swat the cage, but he didn't. Instead he rolled onto his side and spoke to me: I think Haji Jan felt great pain at the end.

Who's to say? I replied. I didn't want to think of Haji Jan's pain.

He was good at the shura, said Mortaza.

He was.

It is a bad thing, he said.

It is.

Do you know what brought me to fight here? asked Mortaza.

I sat up in my bed. You never told me and I never felt I should ask, I replied.

Mortaza laid the switch by his side. He spoke looking past me, towards the cage: It is because the spingaris in my village were foolish just as Haji Jan was. My family used to have a plot of land. Not much, but enough to farm. My father planted wheat and poppy, sometimes almonds. There was always enough. We took what was ours and gave the rest to the spingaris as a tax for the land. This was fair and we were happy. My father would farm and my mother kept house. My sister, very young and dear to my mother, would help her. I helped my father in the fields. We always knew of the war, but it was a far-off thing. When it finally came, groups of fighters arrived in our village. They offered protection to the spingaris in exchange for another tax on the land. We never spoke to these fighters, the spingaris did. They played all the groups off each other, making assurances they

126

could never keep. It was a dangerous game. My family tried to ignore the war. We were happy with our piece of earth, a home, food. It was enough. But this didn't last. Eventually our village was taught that everyone must make a choice.

It was close to the harvest when it happened. I still don't know which group of fighters it was, but my father and I watched from our fields as the mortars fell, one at a time, far-off at first, and then, like the steps of an invisible giant, walking up to our home, stomping it to dust. The two of us ran back and dug through the rubble. We found my mother very quickly. She was still alive. My father screamed over her broken body and I think his spirit died before she did. As we laid her on the ground in her ripped skirts, she lived long enough to ask after my sister, but, thanks to God, not long enough to see me pull her from the tree she'd been blown into. Once I saw her, I rushed into the branches that were familiar from when I'd climbed them as a boy, but it took me another hour to bring her down. By then my father could do nothing but wail over my mother. My sister was only eight years old, small and broken in my arms. And her lips. Blue, so blue.

As he remembered, Mortaza smacked his palm with the switch. He looked down at his high-tops and spoke: I went to the spingaris in my village. I asked them to stand against those that did this, but they refused. They insisted we would suffer more if we took sides. They were cowards, and I told them such. I left and came here, and Commander Sabir promised what the spingaris would not. Now very little grows at our farm. This last season, when my father should've readied for the planting, he instead sowed salt into the furrows, killing the land, denying it to the spingaris or to any other who would lay claim to what's his. He remains in the rubble of our old home. He sits among the broken walls with no roof to protect him, doing no work. He says there is no point. I send him my wage, and that is adequate for survival, but it does nothing for his dead spirit. As for my spirit, I cannot say with certainty who attacked my village. Gazan fighting under the Taliban? Others fighting under Hezb-e-Islami? The Haqqanis? Who knows these things? But what I know is that I've taken a side. I think that is enough.

I sat up and turned towards Mortaza as if to speak, but said nothing. The story of my loss would do nothing to lessen his. Tawas, Qiam, Yar, even Commander Sabir, the burdens of our past led us here, and, alike as we were, we carried those burdens alone.

Through my silence, Mortaza spoke again: But now there is something I must ask you. Do you think we killed Haji Jan today?

What do you mean? I said, not wanting to talk like this.

All of our revenge, he said, our desire for badal at any cost, Commander Sabir's desire to build the outpost . . . do you think all of it killed Haji Jan?

Haji Jan wouldn't choose a side, I replied. This is what killed him, not us.

Yes, not us, he said. We've chosen.

He leaned back onto his bed, picked up the long thin switch, and smacked Puskie's cage. The bird sang: chi-chi-charee, *chi-chi-charee*, CHI-CHI-CHAREE!

I rested against my pillow, stared at the ceiling's wooden planks, and fought to let go of it all, until I managed to let go enough, and to sleep.

★

A few hours later I awoke into a hard silence. I was breathless from a dream I couldn't remember and I didn't feel as though I'd slept at all. Across from me, in the night's mix of light and shadow, Mortaza lay spread on his back, asleep, his high-tops still tied loosely on his feet, the long thin switch still clenched in his hand. I sat up. The rows of beds were no longer empty but heaved, a soldier resting in each one. I needed to piss, and as I left the barracks, I envied the rows of peaceful sleepers, but envy mixed with doubt. There was no reason they should sleep more deeply and soundly than me.

A bright moon strained my tired eyes. It seemed as if I'd stepped into the clearest of days. As clouds floated wide and lazy overhead, shadows moved between the rocks, mixing with the light. I watched the fronts of my boots as I crossed the firebase, struggling not to trip over the uneven ground. But my careful steps caused me to miss my greatest obstacle, Commander Sabir. He gave a sharp whistle. I looked up. Come here, you! he hissed.

He sat on the raised doorway of his tiny plywood shack, squinting into the dark. Light poured from inside and I saw him far better than he saw me. His knees were pulled to his chest. He didn't wear his uniform top, but a white T-shirt, maybe two sizes too large, with a silver Nike Swoosh and the familiar *Just Do It*, printed in black.

Next to his left foot was a bottle of Jim Beam and next to his other foot was a paper cup with a plastic lid. His left arm drooped lazily at his side. In his palm he held the can of fish food. I walked carefully towards him, but my movements weren't quite quick enough. Bacha bazi, come here! he yelled, pointing to me with an outstretched arm. He then looked at his palm, confused, forgetting that in it he clutched the fish food. The discovery of it caused him to laugh into his shoulder.

Commander Sabir tossed the fish food beside the whisky and rose to his feet. I presented myself to him at attention, my arms pinned to my sides and my ankles tucked together. He did the same, and the two of us stood stiff as tin soldiers in front of his door. The night's drinking had already reddened his cheeks to the colour of beef. The rims of his eyes were red, too, and his nose was curled up in a snarl. Where are you going so late? he asked me.

I replied firmly, and in a rhythm, as though clapping the syllables of my words: Commander Sabir, I have to take a piss!

He looked at me. In his eyes was an empty heaviness, like that of a serpent about to strike his meal. His breaths came all from the mouth. A drunken sweat beaded on his forehead. Then, in a blur, his clenched fist flashed towards my face. But he didn't strike. He stopped inches from my nose, tilted his head, and shifted his stare from me to the fist between us. While he considered his fist, he slowly pressed the top of his thumb between his index finger and middle finger so that the tiny nub poked strangely from the knuckles. He wiggled it in the air. Then he tilted his head to the other side, looked past the nub of his thumb to me, and melted into laughter like a boy. Well, go piss then, you fool! he said, and the warm boozy sweetness of his breath blew against my face and a drip of saliva poured from his broken lip, rolling down his shirt front as if it were honey. I walked quickly towards the latrine, but Commander Sabir shouted after me, pointing to the side of his quarters: No! Just piss over there. When you're finished, you'll come drink with me.

He stepped inside to get another paper cup and I stood next to his hut, trying to piss. He called out the door: Who can say I don't care for my soldiers when I share my whisky with them?

I couldn't do it. Commander Sabir's voice and the noise as he searched for another cup made me anxious.

He stepped back outside and sat heavily on his front step. Aren't you done yet? he asked, laughing. Come, put your little nub away, Aziz.

Just a moment, Commander, I replied.

He whistled a hollow and broken tune. I breathed deeply, rolled my shoulders, tried to relax, but nothing came. He stopped whistling and called out: I've fixed you a drink and may have to have it myself if you don't hurry!

I gave up. My bladder still ached, but I buttoned my pants and went to get my drink. I stood in front of him, uncertain where to sit. He patted the doorstep and I settled in next to him as an equal might. Before we drank, he stood, walked inside, and turned out the light. He returned with Omar's glass bowl. He set it on the step between us and the black goldfish circled its waters.

If it is dark, I prefer to have Omar's company, Commander Sabir confessed.

He handed me a paper cup like his. The night was bright with many shadows in it. The shadows fell in Omar's bowl, bending strangely. He seemed to avoid them, weaving through the waters, swimming low and near to the coloured gravel. Watching him, I sipped my drink. It bit and then burned down my throat. I winced against the sweet warmth and stared into my cup. I'd never had alcohol before.

What's a matter? asked Commander Sabir. You don't like it?

No, it's good.

You don't seem to enjoy it, he replied.

I gulped at the whisky and said: I am tired, that's all. Today was difficult.

Bah! he laughed, taking another sip of his drink. He rubbed the back of his neck with a callused palm, looking up, searching for the moon. Its light poured from behind a single cloud. He spoke, and when he did, he did to the moon as much as to me: Today was difficult, but what it really was, was unnecessary. That fool Haji Jan would still be alive if he'd taken my offer. Do you believe me when I tell you this?

Yes, Commander, I said quickly. Of course.

He searched my face as he had done the moon a moment before. He drank some more, saying: Worse than Haji Jan is this fool Atal. He claims to care for his village, but what does he know of such cares? I am responsible for the soldiers here. I care for your broken families. I give you food and a roof. And I give you the chance for badal.

The moon emerged from a cloud and in its light Commander Sabir fumbled at the ground by his feet, searching for Omar's can of fish food.

What of our badal? I asked.

What of it? he replied, still groping at his feet.

We are sick of checkpoints, I said, feeling a new sensation, a warm and slightly drunken courage. We want to strike at Gazan. That is why I came here. That is why we all came here, for badal.

I thought he would grow angry at this, but he said nothing. He found the fish food and opened its lid. The air turned sharp with the smell. He shook the flakes onto the water's surface. They came slowly from the can. Harder and harder he shook, speaking all the while: We do anything for badal because to do nothing is shameful, and shame is feared more than anything. When I killed Hafez and took badal for my brother, I was very afraid.

His voice trailed off. He looked up from the water and held me in his stare.

What will you do after we kill Gazan? he asked.

I'll go back to Orgun, care for my brother, and try to find work.

My words hovered in the air, weightless with all they presumed. Commander Sabir listened and unscrewed the cap from the fish food, blowing through its sieved holes, clearing it. Flakes rose into the air, floating down, dusting my hair and face. He screwed the cap back on. Omar bobbed on the water's surface, his one slick eye winking at me as he waited for his meal.

There are many in the Special Lashkar who've taken badal, said Commander Sabir. Ask Issaq or Yar whether it undoes the pain that has been. Ask them why they're still here, fighting. The war sustains us. It can be a life.

Commander Sabir shook more flakes from the can. They fell into the bowl, a few at a time. Omar ate them one by one. Impatient, Commander Sabir struck the heel of his palm against the can's back. The lid knocked loose, dumping the entire contents into the water. Omar gulped at the food, eating in a frenzy. He would eat until his stomach burst. Bowli! cursed Commander Sabir. He reached into the bowl to scoop out the food, but in his haste, he tipped it to the ground. Water spilled into the dust at our feet. Omar flopped into the mud. Commander Sabir ran inside. I grasped after the fish, snatching him up. His body writhed as I cupped him in my hands. Against my fingertips, I could feel his lips now gulping for air instead of food. Commander Sabir returned with a bottle of water. He poured it into the bowl and I dumped Omar in. Then he stood, holding the bowl up to the moonlight, checking on his pet. Unbothered, Omar went back to eating, sucking the flecks of food buried in the floor of coloured gravel.

Get some rest, said Commander Sabir, there is much to be done. You'll get your chance at badal. Maybe you'll take it, none of that matters unless you've made a life in this war.

He leaned back, emptied his cup of Jim Beam, and wiped his mouth on his sleeve. He tucked the fishbowl under his arm, stumbled into his room, and collapsed on his bed. I closed the door behind him.

My steps were uncertain as I stumbled to the latrine. The moon had carved itself to a sliver and I couldn't tell if my footing faltered because of the darkness or because I'd drunk too much. When I arrived inside, I left the lights off. I straddled the porcelain hole in the ground for a long time before relief finally came. Then I walked back towards the barracks. Commander Sabir's light had been turned back on. I thought of him, drunk, sitting under a single bulb, unable to sleep and, but for his goldfish, afraid of the dark.

I AWOKE THE NEXT MORNING with a headache. Worse than that was the doubt I felt. It promised not to fade so quickly. I thought of all Commander Sabir had said. Even if we killed Gazan, I was trapped. Badal was a clear action, but was it worth my life? It could not change what had happened to my brother, and when I took it, afterwards, I would still know only war.

When Mortaza, Tawas, and I finished breakfast, Yar sat outside on a picnic table waiting. He waved us over and leaned forwards as if in a conspiracy. I have news, he said. Last night after dinner Issaq told me that Commander Sabir knows where to find Gazan and that he has decided to launch a raid against him.

Yar leaned back and studied our blank stares.

Also, he continued, Commander Sabir has decided the Tomahawks will be the assault force for the mission and the Comanches will stay out on the cordon.

Yar cast his palms towards the sky as if he'd just performed a magic trick.

When? asked Mortaza.

Tonight, said Yar.

Tawas slapped Mortaza on the shoulder. Tonight! he said. God is great, truly, He is.

Our badal against Gazan comes tonight, repeated Yar.

Tawas grinned at me with a clean enthusiasm.

I nodded back.

Head to the motor pool, there's work to do, Yar ordered. Details will come later. Commander Sabir wants to ensure that no one has time to warn Gazan. Who knows how many of his spies are among us.

★

For the rest of the morning, I turned a distracted wrench under our HiLux's hood with Tawas. An old air filter had been causing exhaust to rattle through the engine as if it were a pair of tubercular lungs. We struggled to loosen the side bolts and replace the filter. Each time our wrench lost its grip, our knuckles flew into the hard edges of the engine block. Tawas cringed at the pain but smiled to himself.

Why are you so happy? I asked.

This mission, said Tawas, smacking on a piece of his bubblegum. It's what we've waited for.

No part of you is worried?

Not for myself, he said, but I am for Qiam. With me in the assault force, it will be very hard for him to wait on the cordon. And you?

I pushed him aside and turned on the bolt he'd struggled with. Yes, I suppose I am, I muttered, my head under the hood.

You have nothing to worry about. You fought well in the ambush a few weeks ago.

It isn't the raid that makes me nervous, I answered, and tugged hard on the bolt. It came loose. I reached into the space between the engine and the air filter and untwisted it by hand.

I asked: What happens after the raid? Suppose we get Gazan tonight. What happens to us then?

I don't know, said Tawas. Does it truly matter? Maybe I'll stay with the Special Lashkar. Commander Sabir is a fair man. He takes care of us. Gazan isn't the only dog worth killing. There are others. Or, I could try to find work in Orgun, or maybe to the north around FOB Sharana . . . I don't know.

I pulled the old scarred bolt off the air filter. Tawas pushed me out of the way and turned on the next one. All answers don't need to come at once, he said as he thrust his head under the hood. For now badal is enough, and then, well, I believe all will seem as new once Gazan is dead.

His wrench slipped again. His knuckles slammed into the engine block, breaking skin. In pain, he bit his lip, but then smiled to himself, content in his work.

Once Tawas and I replaced the air filter, we walked with the rest of our team to the mess hall. We devoured plates of greasy rice baked into a chalow and warm naan. Back in our barracks, we found Issaq reclining against his bed, full and sleepy. He paid little attention as the squad filed in. Not knowing what to do and not wanting to bother Issaq, Yar motioned for us to sit on our beds and wait. Despite the excitement of what lay ahead, the dust and warm afternoon air ground us towards sleep. Some dozed, and some cleaned rifles and night-vision goggles with old American toothbrushes. All were attuned to the door, though, wondering when Commander Sabir would come with the plan. When finally he entered, it felt like we'd waited a very long time. Silently we stood, wanting to be told what to do and then to do it.

Commander Sabir stopped in the aisle between our bunks. His arms were folded across his Nike Swoosh T-shirt. His skin was pulled tight and pale over his cheeks and chin. Across them was stubble. He looked sick from drinking the night before. At first he spoke quietly to Issaq, who looked down our rows of beds and nodded back. Then Issaq nodded again, raised his arm, and called us over. We silently circled around Commander Sabir.

He turned out his hands and gazed upward, putting his face to God's. Bizmullah ir Rahman ir Rahim, he said in prayer.

We, his soldiers, responded in unison: Bizmullah ir Rahman ir Rahim, in the Name of God, the Compassionate, the Merciful.

Commander Sabir dropped his head, running his palms over his eyes and cheeks. We did the same. He lowered his gaze, levelling his face with ours. A great opportunity has come, he said. This night, Gazan will be at the madrassa along the north road. One of my informants assures me of it. Some spingaris in Gomal have offered to support Gazan with food and weapons. These old fools have planned to meet him so they might discuss this deception, but they will find us there too.

He then explained how the entire Special Lashkar would be part of this raid, how we would capture, and most likely kill, Gazan and the spingaris from Gomal. He described how the Comanches would block the north road and surround the madrassa while we, the Tomahawks, searched its rooms. A simple mission. Commander Sabir handed out some satellite photos he must've gotten from Mr Jack. In them we saw the madrassa, a one-storey square mud building with a high wall running its perimeter. It crowned a round hill that we would run up.

Commander Sabir finished the order and reminded us: The spingaris in Gomal refuse to let us build an outpost. They say they want no part in this war, but they help Gazan. These men are as much our enemies as any.

He finished speaking and in the quiet, he placed his hard stare on each of us. And as he did, I couldn't help but meet his eyes with the glimmer of violent hope in my own.

★

A few hours later, Mortaza shook me by the shoulders.

It is time, he whispered.

Inside the barracks it was dark in that deep way where you must check to see if your eyes are open or closed. I groped next to my bed until I felt my rifle. No one wanted to turn on all the lights. It would be too difficult to shift back into darkness. So we dressed in the dim shadows cast by our flashlights.

It was a little before midnight.

I ran my palms along the barrel of my Kalashnikov and turned on the flashlight bolted to its side. The beam shone a narrow column down the rows of beds where Yar and Tawas stood dressing among the ten others in our squad. They tied black do-rags over their kinked hair, Yar's dark and grey, Tawas's sandy brown. We all shuffled around the barracks, tugging at boots, grabbing rifles and night-vision goggles. I looked over my body armour, my magazines were topped off, my grenade pouches full. I pulled my brother's hospital photo from my cargo pocket. His empty stare made me bitter. It made me bitter enough to be vicious, and I wanted to be vicious. I slid it into a plastic bag and tugged open the Velcro flap on my body armour. I put the photo between the steel plate and the piece of canvas that rested against my chest. If I were shot in front, the round would have to penetrate the steel plate, then the photo, and then my body. I draped my body armour over my head. It fell heavily against me and, as thin as the photo was, I felt it on my chest.

Yar was the first to leave our barracks for the trucks. The rest of our team followed. As we stepped outside, a strong wind blew smooth and warm against our bodies, and the clouds were low in the sky and heavy with rain. Across the firebase, Commander Sabir paced inside his quarters, his silhouette breaking the light that leaked out around his door frame. He readied himself for the darkness. Past his quarters, the night was complete. The moon had yet to rise and we shuffled through the rocky dirt, kicking up invisible dust that we breathed and tasted.

At the motor pool, we searched for our HiLux until Tawas found it in the darkness. He opened the back door, climbed in, and flashed his light once for the rest of us to see. No one spoke. We took our positions. I climbed over the tailgate to the machine gun. My foot caught, sending me face-first into the bed.

You all right, Aziz? asked Tawas.

Fine, I said between clenched teeth. Then I noticed that the flashlight bolted to my Kalashnikov's side had been knocked loose. I reached blindly for it in the bed, but we had no time to spare. It was lost.

From inside the cab, I could hear the radio on the dash and the noise of its transmissions as they came and went in static. Our HiLux jerked into gear, and we drove towards the gate where the rest of the convoy assembled. Yar lined up our truck in the column. Some of the Comanches had already gone to block the north road. The rest of them, two HiLuxes' worth, were lined up in front of us. Their engines idled and they gathered in small groups outside their vehicles. A single soldier peeled off from one of the groups and jogged down the convoy. He first stopped at Commander Sabir's HiLux, which had parked just ahead of us. The soldier looked closer and saw the two Afghan flags on the hood, flapping in the night breeze. He ran past the truck. Just as he did, Commander Sabir stepped out from it. Yar saw him and went to see what he wanted, soon joined by Issaq and the Comanches' squad and team leaders.

While Yar jogged towards Commander Sabir, the soldier continued to jog towards us until he hooked his arms over our HiLux's bed and looked up at me. His night-vision goggles covered his face, but in a familiar voice he called out: Is this Tawas's truck?

It was Qiam. I lifted my goggles so he could see me, but when my naked eyes looked back at him, his face disappeared into the darkness. It's me, Aziz, I said. Tawas is in the cab.

Qiam grasped my arm. Aziz! he cried. Good luck tonight, my friend!

He opened the back door and climbed inside. The wind whipped across our convoy and the clouds hung increasingly low. A few moments later Mortaza stepped from the cab. He looked up at me and called out above the wind: The brothers should have a moment to speak before a thing such as this.

Mortaza and I stood silently and listened to the rhythm of their hushed conversation. I looked out over our convoy. The Comanches' trucks idled in front of us. The two red stripes marking their doors, Mr Jack's war paint, appeared dark and green in my tiny field of view. The first of their two HiLuxes was parked with its fender eagerly pressed against the gate – the lead vehicle. Our assault element was lined up behind them – our squad's two HiLuxes and Commander Sabir's. I watched him as he stood in his huddle with Issaq, Yar, and the others. His hands rested solidly on his hips. The figures around him gestured wildly, their arms flapping like streamers on the wind, making their arguments. And while their debate continued, Commander Sabir stood motionless. Then he pointed once at Yar, said something, and pointed at the convoy. The group walked back to their trucks.

I banged on top of the cab. Qiam stepped outside and Mortaza climbed into his seat. Make him suffer, Qiam shouted over the wind. Tawas's arm reached through his open window and grasped his brother's. Then their grips broke and Qiam jogged back up the convoy. There was a great love between the two. It came from lives spent suffering together. And for me, it was a sad thing to think that but for their suffering, they would not have been so close.

I pulled apart the Velcro on my body armour. My fingers found the photo of my brother pressed against my chest. My breaths rose and fell against the steel plate, anxious and quick.

Without Ali, I was alone.

Yar ran back to our truck. Aziz, he said, the plan has changed. There is a back door to the madrassa, and from the cordon in the hills, the Comanches won't be able to see it. When we arrive you'll move quickly to the far side and cover the door. Shoot any who run from it.

Any? I asked.

Any! Yar shouted above the wind. All who run are against us. Hold your position until I wave you inside.

Yar disappeared into the cab to explain the new plan. Up front the Comanches' trucks shifted into gear and our convoy unspooled onto the high plain. Once the Comanches left, all that remained was Commander Sabir's HiLux in front of us and Issaq's behind us. Although there were nearly thirty soldiers on the operation, there would be barely ten of us in the assault. I felt exposed and, for the first time since I'd arrived in Shkin, truly afraid. Then Commander Sabir's HiLux shifted into gear and bounced towards the north road and the madrassa. As we followed him, the firebase's steel gate crashed shut behind us.

I sat in the bed of the truck and held on to the buttstock of my machine gun. The moon wouldn't rise until almost morning and we sank deeper and deeper into the darkness and the mountains. Our convoy kicked up dust. Nothing appeared clear. I focused and refocused my night-vision goggles. Behind us, Issaq's HiLux trailed like a spirit. Every few minutes its headlights and fender would float in front of me, glowing like a mouth and eyes swimming in dust and night. When we'd approach a steep climb or cross a wide ravine the HiLux would slip farther behind, disappearing like a face submerged in clouded waters.

After an hour or so, a flash of small lights appeared ahead of us on the north road. I flipped up my goggles but saw nothing. I put them back down and they reappeared. They were infrared. The Comanches' first set of checkpoints. I stared past the hood of our truck. The lights grew brighter and brighter, pulsing, yet invisible to all except us.

A single HiLux was parked on the narrow shoulder. A soldier climbed from its cab, his rifle slung across his back, but without his body armour, night-vision goggles, or helmet. He'd taken off the cumbersome equipment. Without it, he seemed naked. Through the darkness he glanced towards us. His eyes mirrored the light like some sort of night animal, his face appeared dim and hollow. He couldn't see the road, but he could hear us on it. We drove towards him, but he stared past us and into the mountain range beyond. Without his goggles he'd chosen to be blind and to find more of the world in what he could not see.

Commander Sabir's HiLux stopped just before the checkpoint. He climbed out of the driver's seat and shouted into the wind. The soldier came to attention and ran towards a single strand of concertina wire that blocked the road. By instinct his hands found the wire and slid it clear. Commander Sabir's HiLux shifted back into gear, its flags caught the wind, and our convoy drove past the checkpoint and farther down the north road. As we passed, the soldier waved and gave us a victory sign, but still he stared, unseeing, into the darkness of the mountains.

It started to drizzle and the wind rose and a warm summer rain came down in sheets. It was loud against the earth. I couldn't understand the transmissions inside the cab, but I could hear the static from Yar's radio key in and out, in and out. My anticipation grew. At any moment our HiLux would stop, its doors would fly open, and we'd lead our assault over the steep ground to the madrassa. The rain was lucky. It would mask the sound of our movements, but still we would need to run fast. Perched on one of the ammunition cans, I stretched my legs in front of me and kneaded at their muscles with the heel of my palm. Behind our HiLux, a circle of lights flickered and formed among the ridgelines above. I flipped up my goggles. My naked eyes saw only blackness. The lights were infrared, the inner cordon, the Comanches. Almost there.

The rising moon shone full and bright behind clouds that glowed almost orange. We turned off the main road and down a smooth ribbon in the mud that suggested a trail. It ran hardly a hundred yards up the hill and towards the madrassa. Soon our convoy crammed fender to bumper along it and Commander Sabir's HiLux shuddered and stopped. His door swung open. He shouted against the wind that came hard over the mountains, but I couldn't hear him. Our HiLux came to a sudden halt and my chest slammed against the cab. I was glad for the steel plate I wore and I thought of the photo of my brother pressed between it and my chest. I leapt over the tailgate and landed hard on the ground. As I stood, Tawas scrambled around the back and pulled a wooden scaling ladder from the bed. He ran with one arm hooked through its rungs and the other grasping his rifle. Issaq and Yar formed the assault element into a line whose width faced the madrassa. Tawas and the ladder arrived, the final missing piece. Then the entire string of us fanned out and advanced up the hill, its roundness crowned by the square-walled madrassa.

I trotted heavily up the slope and my feet slipped in the mud. Twice I fell. Yar pointed wildly for me to break off and find the madrassa's back entrance. I advanced a bit more with the raiding party and then crossed the face of the hill, alone, towards its farthest and darkest side. I ran with the moonlight behind me. It cast a long shadow against my path. The contrast of light and shadow made seeing more of a challenge than in the pure night. After only a few steps, I rolled my ankle. I glanced over my shoulder. Behind me the rest of the raid force made good progress towards the madrassa. I ran atop my shadow and slowly the cordon of lights in the mountains dissolved. I fell heavily into the mud. I pushed myself up and looked over my shoulder once more. A figure – Tawas or Mortaza? – stood on the scaling ladder's highest rung and leapt over the madrassa's outer wall. Then the front gate crashed open and the assault force streamed inside. The warm wind mixed with their muted shouts, becoming like a single noise. Flashlights blinked on and off in the compound, shining against the rain. I still hadn't reached the back door. Ignoring the uneven ground, I ran faster. Just ahead the mountain blocked the moonlight. I crossed into that farthest and darkest shadow. Here my footing became more assured. The moonlight no longer conspired against me. The twinkling cordon of the surrounding mountaintops disappeared.

I knew I should be able to see the back door. And then I saw it, barely. It swung open, a darker piece of darkness blown by the wind. Someone ran out of it. I glimpsed the figure, sprinting in a crouch and then dipping over the hilltop, gone. I was too late. Had I missed Gazan? I heard the door slam hard, twice, but looking at it, it hadn't moved. Then I realised the slams were not the door but gunshots. I threw myself on my stomach and strained to see the door. Whatever came from it next, I would not miss. My fingers slid up my Kalashnikov towards my flashlight, but touched nothing. I squinted through my goggles, seeing very little through the rain. Suddenly a darkened blur pushed open the door. Three times I fired at it. I took the first two shots quickly, without aiming. I paused, calmed myself, and aimed for the third. Then I squinted again, and there was just the door and the wind in the rain.

I breathed, my stomach against the mud. Small rocks pushed at my legs. I waited. I didn't know if I'd killed the man, but I'd done something. How long I lay there was difficult to say, but I remained long enough to think that perhaps I'd killed someone I would be proud to kill. A light flashed from inside the compound and out the back door. It flashed off almost immediately. There was a long moment of indecision. The light did nothing more. Then came a shout: Aziz, are you out there!

It was Yar.

I am here! I yelled back.

Come and help me! Something was wrong. His voice was frightened. I ran up the hill. The dark side of the compound and the tops of the ridgelines were deep blue in the not-quite-morning light. I could now see the door I'd been watching. It was made of tin and covered in a peeling mural – a rich and festive mountain range with green valleys and a blue stream running through its heart. The door creaked on its hinges in the wind, banging against the tan suede boot of the man I'd killed, and the sound seemed like a slow steady knocking on the door of all the unhappiness I would ever know.

I took off my helmet and threw it and the attached night-vision goggles into the abundant pool around Tawas's head. The canvas on his body armour was torn open at the chest and the steel plate inside was darkly singed and twice dented. His helmet was gone and underneath his right eye was a small hole, no bigger than a pebble. Sandy-brown curls ringed from beneath his black do-rag that matched the one worn by Yar, who stood over him. The curls lay cleanly across his ashen, almost green, forehead, which was furrowed and frozen with the surprised look that bound the moment between my first two shots hitting his body armour and the third hitting his cheek.

Yar tugged under Tawas's arms and tried to drag him out of the rain and into the compound. But when Yar dragged him, he came apart. The back of his head leaked everywhere. Still, Yar pulled. A chewed piece of bubblegum fell from Tawas's mouth and mixed with what spilled from his head. And now everything blended with the mud and all parts were lost in it. Seeing this, Yar couldn't stand the pulling any longer. Across the doorway's skirt, he set Tawas down. He then ran into the compound. While he did, I stood next to my friend as the wind tried to close the tin door against his body.

Yar returned with a thick fleece blanket he'd taken from one of the small mud-walled rooms that lined the madrassa's courtyard. He draped it across the top half of Tawas, leaving his legs and boots sticking horribly in the air. Now that the head had been covered, Yar wiped his face with a tired hand. What happened? he asked, and I think I was crying.

No one was supposed to come out the back door, I said.

How could you have mistaken him? he demanded.

Again I said: No one was supposed to come out the back door.

My voice had become broken and angry, my response unsatisfying but true. It was not my fault. *No one was supposed to come out the back door.* Inside, lights flashed wildly against the compound walls. Silhouettes wove among each other, full of purpose, as the search for Gazan continued. Then one of the silhouettes stood over Yar and me.

Commander Sabir looked down at the pile under the blanket. He considered it for a moment and volleyed his gaze between us. The trucks will pull up here in a few minutes, he mumbled dryly. Load it in the back with you, Aziz. He shook his head at me and spoke to Yar firmly: Keep your eyes on him. All will be dealt with when we return.

A rush of blood rose from my stomach to my face and the permanence of my mistake settled warmly in my cheeks.

Commander Sabir turned from us and supervised the rest of the search. Two blank-eyed men with wide unbalanced faces, brothers, it seemed, stood in the middle of the madrassa's courtyard. The one man's blue and the other man's white shalwar kameez were mud-stained from where they'd been pushed to the ground and searched. A cluster of children clung to their legs. Parked next to the children and these two teachers was a white binjo, dented and old. Across from it was a white HiLux with a silver lightning bolt across the side. I recognised the HiLux immediately – Atal's. Issaq recognised it too. He stuck his finger, dyed with henna, in the faces of the two strange-looking teachers as he spat questions at them.

What time did these trucks get here?

The men stared dumbly at each other, and the swarm of children tucked themselves tighter and tighter against their legs.

Issaq asked again.

They came after we were asleep, said the man in blue, his words tangling.

Sometimes they come at night. Who are we to ask the reason? added the man in white, his voice equally twisted against some defect of his birth.

Issaq threw open the binjo's trunk.

Mortaza stepped from one of the rooms on the far side of the madrassa. He helped Issaq empty the contents of the binjo into the courtyard. Blankets, pans, a change of clothes, and even a machine gun landed on the ground. Then Mortaza and Issaq hoisted out two large bags of rice with the familiar USAID stencilling. The heaps fell flatly in the mud and pushed each of us into our own thoughts and suspicions. Commander Sabir walked over, glanced down, and considered the bags of rice.

Bring our trucks around, he said with a snarl, his eyes meeting no one's. It is time to go.

What about the HiLux and the binjo? asked Issaq.

We don't have enough drivers to take them, said Commander Sabir as he walked off. He then stopped, turned back at us, and said: But take the rice, Issaq. Have your men load those bags.

Mortaza ran to the base of the hill where our HiLux was parked. Yar and I pulled the bags out of the binjo. We heaved them across the madrassa's courtyard and set them next to the blanketed heap that was Tawas. We pondered the bags and the heap. They were like a jigsaw puzzle we'd have to fit into the bed of our truck.

We'll need to get his body armour off, said Yar, rubbing the back of his neck.

I nodded and Yar kept rubbing at his neck, staring at the pieces and wondering how they might all fit.

We could roll him tightly in the blanket and load him into the bed, I said. Without the armour he'll be lighter, and in the blanket less mess.

Yar scowled at me. My suggestions weren't welcome.

He breathed heavily towards the sky, and then in the same manner towards his feet. Still, he rubbed his neck and stared at the heap on the ground. Get him out of his body armour, he said. Roll him up in the blanket and load him in that way.

I nodded and tried not to show any unwelcome emotion as I pulled back the blanket. The blood, which still had enough life in it to clot, stuck against the fleece's fur. It peeled from the head and body as if it were glue that had yet to dry. Smelling the blood, a pair of black- and white-feathered magpies landed in the mud next to Tawas. Their jutting heads considered him for a moment. They came no farther. As I looked at the two birds, they looked at me, stomping their fine talons into the earth. I wondered if they'd sing for me. Chi-chi-charee, chi-chi-charee. They were silent. Perhaps not all birds sing like Puskie. Who would care for him now? My throat thickened, thinking of all I'd taken from my friend. Such ideas were useless. Silly as birds. I grabbed the blanket's sopping corners and whipped it in the air. The magpies spooked, their blue wingtips fluttering against the slate sky. I smoothed the blanket's ends with my hands and turned back to the body. Pinned beneath two heavy dead legs was Tawas's rifle. I picked up the slick barrel between my fingers and tossed it aside. Mud stuck to it like batter to meat. I tugged at the Velcro flaps that ran under each arm, unfastening the body armour. The first flap opened with a dry scraping hiss and the second separated with a silent, easy wetness. I unfolded the vest like a door with hinges set at the shoulders. Underneath the armour, the uniform was soaked in sweat that was still warm. I stood by the pulpy head and reached my arms under its back, where the soil mixed wet and doughy between my fingers. I heaved with my legs and the body flopped face-first onto the outspread blanket. I rolled the whole mess up and looked at Yar. He averted his eyes, focusing instead on Mortaza and his progress towards our HiLux at the bottom of the hill. Yar must have felt my gaze on him because he glanced at the blanket and nodded his approval. I crouched to the ground and washed my sticky hands in the mud.

It had stopped raining by the time Mortaza pulled up in our HiLux. Issaq's and Commander Sabir's trucks had also arrived. The hilltop filled with the noise of many idling engines. Tired soldiers collapsed into their seats. Sets of clear little eyes peeked at us from cracks in the wood shutters that lined the madrassa. The children and their two teachers waited for our departure. Looking at them, I imagined a different life, one where Ali and I attended a madrassa like this, where I still had a mother and father, where a day like Ashura would remind me of visits home from school instead of a destroyed home.

Mortaza grabbed my shoulder. Silently, he thumbed towards the bed of our truck.

Body first? I asked.

Mortaza nodded back.

We crammed the blanketed heap into the bed, but it was too tall to fit. We pushed against it. Stiffly, it folded, knees to chest, into the position of a sleeping infant. We loaded the bags of rice around the body. When we slammed the tailgate shut there was no room in the bed for anything else, so I opened the door to the cab, to where Tawas used to sit. As I did, Yar and Mortaza both watched me. I stopped, thought better of it, and climbed into the back, to where the body rested, my usual space.

Lying there, its knees tucked into its chest, the blanket looked human, like Tawas. I leaned my rifle against the cab, near where his arms were. I thought he might reach through the blanket, grab the rifle, and make things even between us. I still hadn't made a space for myself when Yar shifted into gear and we started towards Shkin. As we pulled away from the madrassa, the children and their teachers walked into the courtyard and stood stupidly next to the white HiLux and binjo we'd left behind. Their confused faces struggled to understand what had happened, just like mine. I sat down and made a seat of Tawas's hips.

III

I FELT NUMB. On the journey back I waited for a rush of emotion that never came. When we returned from the raid, Commander Sabir took my rifle and confined me to Naseeb's quarters. He was worried about my safety, or at least the mess Qiam would make if he took badal.

Commander Sabir slammed the door behind me, leaving poor Naseeb out in the dirt wearing only shower shoes, underpants, and a T-shirt. I felt very bad for him, much more so than for Qiam or Tawas. Towards the brothers I once called friends I felt a strange emptiness. What I'd done to Tawas, and what Qiam might do to me, was the source of all my troubles. Should I feel pity for Qiam, even though his badal now threatened my life? Had I lost all compassion? I fought to avenge my brother, but I'd just killed the brother of another man, a friend. I'd taken from him just what Gazan had taken from me. Had I become the very thing I despised, that which I wished to destroy?

The door locked from the outside. I had nowhere to go so I climbed onto Naseeb's mattress and sank into the large rut he'd worn in the weak foam. The wood bed frame pushed against my back. My legs went numb, all pins and needles. I wanted to hold on to the sensation. I didn't want to feel anything. Then I fell asleep.

In the dark morning, I heard the lock turn and awoke with a start. The lights flipped on and Commander Sabir stood in front of me, silhouetted by the hut's open door. Quickly, he closed it.

Relax, he said. You have nothing to fear from me.

I propped myself on my elbows and leaned against the headboard. Commander Sabir sat at the foot of my mattress like a father putting his child down to sleep. He looked at the ceiling and tapped his silver ring on the bed frame a few times.

What a mess we have. What a mess.

I couldn't have known, I answered. No one was supposed to come out the back door.

Just as I finished, Commander Sabir sprang from the bed and raised himself up, his chest and fist lifting in the air. Before I could cover my head, he pummelled me across its side. I collapsed to the floor. My left ear rang. I took a breath, but it came as a gasp. A spike of pain ran up the base of my skull. I opened my eyes. The toes of Commander Sabir's boots were at my face. Around them, flickering, I saw spots, white pinholes, my mind out of focus. He grasped under my armpits and gently lifted me up.

Careful, Aziz, careful, he said as if he'd had no part in knocking me down.

I'm sorry, Commander, I muttered.

He helped me onto the side of the bed. We sat next to each other. My head throbbed. I remembered the soldier who'd gotten Issaq's HiLux stuck in the ravine many weeks before. Commander Sabir had struck him in much the same way, breaking his nose. What I feared in Commander Sabir wasn't his capacity for cruelty but his capacity for kindness, or what seemed like kindness. The true violence in him was the way he moved between the two, caring for my brother's needs while pummelling me. To be his friend was as dangerous as to be his enemy.

He patted my leg, shaking his head. I know you're sorry, he said. But you have made a mess. I've already sent a convoy north with Qiam and the body. You must leave before he returns. I can't say if he'll swear badal against you, but if he does, it can't be taken on my firebase.

A warm anxiety poured from my stomach into my limbs. It was like my livelihood bleeding from me. How would I care for my brother in Orgun if I left the Special Lashkar? And if I went to Orgun, Qiam could easily find me there. I needed to leave, but how and to where? I imagined myself again wandering through some brown guttered alley, eking out a living but without my brother. My situation silently slid towards destitution and Commander Sabir sat on my bed and watched, tapping his ring against the bed frame, faster and faster.

You've always been a good soldier, he said.

I have.

Yes, and it shouldn't end this way for you.

It shouldn't.

I have a proposal so it won't. Would you like to hear it? He smiled at me as though I'd already accepted, which perhaps I had. He explained: There is something more troubling than what happened with Tawas. At the madrassa you saw, just as I did, Atal's truck parked alongside Gazan's and you saw, just as I did, our supplies sitting inside. I've often wondered how Gazan's men stole these things. Naseeb is an incompetent, but this never fully explained it. Tonight it became clear. Atal has deceived us. He steals our supplies when he meets the American here. He claims to oppose our outpost because he wants Gomal kept from the fighting, but his true motive is to support Gazan.

So what would you have me do? I asked.

Commander Sabir nodded with respect.

Atal has a certain fondness towards you, he said. I've seen it. After we speak, you will be discharged from the Special Lashkar. This will be expected. You must then leave here and find Atal. He won't turn his back to you. See what you can learn about his activities. In exchange for this information, I will ensure that your brother remains cared for at the hospital.

I let the proposal sink in for a moment. Commander Sabir knew I had no other choice, I had to support Ali, but he added a final point: This is an opportunity for us both. Depending on the nature of Atal's deceit, this situation might allow you to find Gazan and take your badal.

A jolt of excitement charged up my spine. I levelled my eyes on Commander Sabir's. To be an informant was shameful, thieving others' secrets, but the opportunity to strike at Gazan had nang. Slowly I nodded.

With all respect, I said, how will I know my brother is cared for once I've gone to Gomal?

Commander Sabir's top lip unrolled into a self-satisfied grin.

First get rid of the uniform, he replied. I'll get you some regular clothes. Also, you'll be given this month's pay and next's. That should be enough to figure a way down to the village. When you get there, buy a new phone and I'll give you a number where you can reach me. Memorise it. Don't write it down or save it. As for Ali's care, well, you must trust me in that.

If I want to quit? I asked.

That won't be done. Ours is a partnership.

His smile was broad and appealing.

Yes, a partnership, I replied, and we shook.

Naseeb will drop off some clothes and escort you to the gate, he said. Recite this number from memory when you depart.

He held out a slip of paper. I took it. As I did, he patted me on the leg and left, locking the door behind him. I sat on the edge of the bed. It was still dark outside. My head ached from where Commander Sabir had struck me. I was tempted to turn out the light, to go back to sleep, and to forget, forget everything. I couldn't get dressed, I didn't yet have the clothes I'd change into. And I couldn't sleep, not with this challenge laid before me. I sat under the lights, reciting the number 09973285676, waiting.

Sometime later – a few minutes, hours? – the lock turned again and Naseeb's silhouette appeared in the door. He still wore only his shower shoes and underwear. He also carried a brown shalwar kameez in unopened plastic packaging. I imagined stacks of fresh clothing in his supply locker, folded and ready for these occasions. It occurred to me that I wasn't the only informant. I'd begun a new game, one played with another set of rules.

Do you need anything else? Naseeb asked, and there was pain in his voice.

No, I said, changing my clothes. Just take me to the front gate.

Outside the moon was still up, its silver light running deep blue among the rocks and the rooftops. My aching head eased. As we approached the gate, Naseeb hung back, darkly, as though he were my executioner. I turned over my shoulder and he gave me a strained grin. We had been friends, after all, in that way you only realise once the friendship is over. And to him this entire event, the details of which he didn't understand, added another link to the chain of violent disappointments that were his life in Shkin. Just before we reached the gate, he touched the back of my arm and spoke: Good luck, Aziz. I hope where you go, you go well.

I nodded, not certain if the luck he wished was for my protection or for the success of a mission he didn't understand but sensed. I walked closer to the gate. Its distant image came into focus in the moonlight. Only one person stood at it and the sentry towers were empty. Before I could see him, I heard Commander Sabir's ring tapping against the steel gate arm. He heaved it up and pressed his face close to mine, searching for a final assurance that my mind was clear.

09973285676, I said.

He smiled back and closed the gate.

*

The firebase sat atop a hill that was pale in the near-dawn. I slowly walked to its base and stood on the flat north road. Its hard-packed gravel felt stable beneath my feet. It had been built with a logic and ran as a single ribbon of such towards Gomal.

I knew I'd never finish the journey on foot, but still I walked, putting distance between the firebase and myself, enough distance that I might imagine how to approach Atal when I arrived. Soon dawn broke and a steady stream of cars and motorcycles came down the road. I waved to each as it passed, but I was still too close to our firebase and none would stop. I walked half the day before a vehicle pulled over, and then my challenge became one of negotiation.

Can you give me a ride? I'd say. Depends, how much do you have? they'd ask. Enough, I'd tell them. To where, they'd want to know. Then I'd say: I'm going to Gomal. This I cannot do, they'd answer. Or they'd reply: You will need to pay me more than that!

It grew late. I now walked along one of the many thin footpaths that spread across the mountains as veins do from a distant heart. Behind me there was a faint motor, and with it, a tall dust wisp that travelled at angles through the ridges.

As the wisp cornered the bend nearest me, I saw it was from a motorbike. The driver bounced heavily along the uneven path. The steel of his shock springs slapped against each other at the coils. I waved broadly above my head, flagging him down. He pulled up next to me and a cloud of white dust kicked up around us. We stood in this moment of fog until an unhurried breeze carried it off.

The driver was fat, but not in a deliberate way. Beneath his fat was a muscled strength. It suggested an old power he seldom used. His eyes were grey and glimmered loose as water on a steel plate. His turban's running end was pulled across his face to keep the dust from his mouth. He untucked it and I recognised him. It was the spingari Mumtaz, whom I'd seen in the shura.

What type of a fool walks in these mountains this close to night? he asked, seeming not to remember me.

I need help getting to Gomal, I said. I'm looking for work there.

What work is there in a village that is being strangled? he answered.

I tensed, realising the improbability of my story. Concern must have been written across my face because Mumtaz tilted his motorbike straight, ready to continue on his way.

I can pay you! I pleaded.

He eased his weight back. The points of his grey moustache looked like the points of two tears and he pulled at their drips, speaking: Am I to understand that you are a man with money who looks for work in a village where there is no work? Where will you stay when you arrive?

I hadn't thought of that, I said.

This is some journey you're on! answered Mumtaz. He leaned back in his seat, laughing with a fullness that caused the front tyre of his motorbike to ease from the ground. Come, he said, settling back down. I own a small inn. It's more of an extra room really, but business has been bad. If you have money, I'll earn it. If you stay with me while you find work, I'll help you on your journey. But don't say you were not warned. Finding work will take very long.

My name is Aziz, I said, and offered my hand.

Mumtaz, he answered, and wrapped his palm around mine. The nubs of his fingers were a gristle of fat and muscle, and he hoisted me onto his motorbike. We continued heavily down the trail, rushing ahead of the night.

For the entirety of our trip, I clenched the sides of the back-seat. I strained over Mumtaz's wide shoulders to see what lay ahead. Each time I did this, the motorbike lost its balance and tilted dangerously to one side or the other. Night came quickly, but Mumtaz refused to let the darkness slow him. On our route we passed a few dim cooking fires that flickered against mud-brick walls. Eventually few became many and we arrived.

Mumtaz stopped and turned off the ignition. The streets were empty at this late hour and the clean silence of the moun-tains rang in my ears. We both stretched our backs towards the sky, very black and pricked by the light of many stars. I helped Mumtaz push the motorbike through a gate in the heavy mud wall that surrounded his inn. We leaned the motorbike against a stick-and-wire coop. As we did, an animal thrashed inside, startling me.

That's Iskander, laughed Mumtaz. He feels at home with the chickens.

A white-and-brown dog with clipped ears poked out his neck, canted his head, and, making little of me, returned to the coop. Mumtaz stopped outside the main house, turned at a sickly generator's hand crank, and stepped inside. A low mechanic hum brought the night air alive and put me at ease.

In the house, Mumtaz flipped on a switch that hung from an exposed wire. It connected to a single lightbulb that dangled from a nail, rusted and bent. It had been hammered into a petrified beam of pine that was set into the ancient roof of thatch and mud. Mumtaz's thick hands pulled from a pile of dry branches neatly stacked in the corner. He fed them into a tin stove that sat in the centre of the house's single room. Its chimney was made of hollowed cooking-oil cans that led through a hole in the roof just next to the beam. The fire creaked and smoke leaked from the stove's mouth. Mumtaz slammed the door shut and the room warmed. The two of us sat next to the stove, quiet and weary from travel. I didn't want to ask if I would stay in this room or in the coop with Iskander. In his own time Mumtaz would tell me.

He crawled stiffly along the floor, leaving his legs crossed. He dragged over a shopping bag full of pistachios crusted in salt. He placed the bag between us and ate them from his fists, cracking the shells between the knuckles of one hand. Still we didn't speak, and as the pile of shells grew to a mound, I realised this was dinner. At one point Mumtaz chuckled to himself, as I noticed he was fond to do. He mumbled: You were going to walk down here for work, wonderful! Then he stood, swept the mound of shells into his palms, and threw them into the fire. He unfolded a foam mattress with a red-and-blue Persian print. He lay on it and pulled a fleece blanket over his head. I gazed at this blanketed heap and he seemed lessened. The home was not an inn, and there was no extra room, except for this room shared by the two of us, but there was company. Mumtaz wanted some and for that I was grateful. I stood, turned off the light, and slept on the floor with nothing.

The night was cold, and all through it, I got up, stepped lightly over Mumtaz, and fed dried branches into the mouth of the stove. Once the last scrap burned out in the fire, a chill set into my legs and woke me. I walked into the compound's dirt court-yard to wait for the dawn. As the early light came, I saw how poor Mumtaz was. His home was nothing more than the small coop, the mud room we slept in, and the four walls of the courtyard. A ditch ran beneath one of the walls and out the back. Dishes were stacked alongside it. This was the kitchen. Past Mumtaz's compound were the mountains. Though it seemed these never ended, they were not enough to protect the village from the war, but they were enough to preserve it — it and its traditions. And, even as isolated as the village was, sprouts of progress had arrived: motorbikes, cell phones, and a few homemade satellite dishes that perched from rooftops, all standing as messengers from other, more modern, worlds. But it was a false progress. It measured not movement forwards, but the distance we would soon travel backward when the war destroyed everything.

Just to the east, the border traced the summits of the moun-tains. Soon the sun would rise there. Already its snow-covered ridges throbbed deep blue like a first sky. These peaks were the only ones that stood tall enough to still have snow. Just beneath them, the pines bit their roots into the rocky soil. Somewhere among those peaks or beyond them were Gazan's men. Looking towards the border, I felt my wish for badal mix with my wish for redemption, for what I did to Tawas.

I opened Mumtaz's front gate and craned my neck into the dirt lane outside. I wished to see Gomal again, but not as I had before, not as a soldier. Mud-walled homes ran along the lane for a few hundred yards and emptied into a bazaar that was nothing more than a gathering of wood stalls and steel-shuttered mud huts. One by one, columns of smoke rose from the thatched rooftops as cooking fires were lit.

I heard a hacking cough behind me and a tired shuffling of feet. Mumtaz stepped through the courtyard and landed on his knees by the pots and pans. He pulled down the band of his trousers and pissed into the ditch that ran out the back wall. The kitchen was also the toilet. Iskander trotted from the chicken coop and licked Mumtaz behind the ears. He reached back, patted the dog on the head, and groaned. Then he stood heavily, planting one leg after the other as if he were summiting a mountain.

Good morning, I trust you slept well? he asked.

Very well, thank you, I said.

He poured a pitcher into a steel dish, rinsing it, and then he tossed the dirty water into the ditch so it guttered beneath the back wall with his piss.

Come, he said. I'll fix us some breakfast.

He offered a smile that was impossible not to return. I carried an armful of wood from the chicken coop to the stove and restarted the fire. This and the rising sun heated the room quickly. Mumtaz came through the doorway with a bag of rice, an onion, and a steel pot of water. We boiled the rice, cut the onion, and waited for our breakfast to cook. Each time Mumtaz opened the lid and stirred, he inhaled the steamy smells of our meal, making a great show of his preparations.

Food has been very tough to come by since the checkpoints, he said. But you're my meelma. Let no man say that Mumtaz doesn't understand hospitality.

You've been very gracious, I said, and thanked him.

You'll need your strength if you're going to find work here, he answered, laughing.

I said nothing to this, but asked: Will I be able to buy a phone in the bazaar?

Oh, yes, he said, there are several vendors there who can help you.

I could sense Mumtaz's curiosity, but manners would keep him from asking whom I'd be calling, so I answered his curiosity with a lie. Good, I said, my family will be glad to know I've arrived and am looking for work.

Mumtaz returned an unsatisfied nod.

As we waited for our meal to cook, we sat silently. I thought about the phone, and as I did I recited Commander Sabir's number in my head: *09973285676, 09973285676, 09973285676*. It had become like a prayer, uttered often, tethering me to my purpose.

Mumtaz heaped two spoons' worth of rice into my steel bowl. I took large mouthfuls and ate quickly. I wanted to finish before he did and leave for the bazaar, alone. If I travelled with him, the people in the village would be more likely to approach me. I wondered if my story would unravel against their questions. The thought of it reminded me of the nervousness I once felt when repeating my multiplication tables to Ali. I hoped to avoid that pressure. In the bazaar I'd figure out a way to get a phone, but more important, I'd figure out a way to get to Atal.

I finished breakfast and took my dish out to the kitchen as I left. Iskander saw me pass through the gate and into the dirt lane. With me gone, he ran inside to be with Mumtaz as the meal was finished.

The streets came to life with a slow pulse. A few men walked towards the bazaar, pushing wheelbarrows or carrying items of little value – wood, scrap metal, some old electronics. Others did nothing at all. They crouched in their doorways and watched the day pass as if its possibility were a rumour. Behind them, through the open gates of their compounds, women cleaned. They washed linens in water basins and dried their many-coloured wraps of green, red, and blue on the cracked mud walls. At times, the wind caught these colours and the inside walls billowed into a bright festival while the colour of the outside walls seemed lost to the earth. Many of the women stared at me from their homes as I passed. Their faces were uncovered and drawn to my unknown face by instinct. And despite all, Gomal endured, it stirred with a determination to exist, despite Commander Sabir's siege, despite Gazan's mortar attacks, and despite Atal's stubbornness.

I walked through the village carefully. I met no one's stare, but neither did I look away. If I were seen, perhaps it would come to the attention of Atal and he'd find me, but if I were noticed, my purpose might be questioned. All things were balance in this new game.

When I arrived at the bazaar, most of the stalls had just opened. A man with a clean white shalwar kameez and a neat grey vest raised the rolled steel shutter of his shop front. Inside was a well-kept display of electronics.

Can I help you? he asked, his voice flat and unwelcoming.

I'm looking for a mobile, I said.

The man fastened a lock that held the steel shutter open and its weight sagged against the mud wall to which it was bolted. He disappeared behind a wooden counter, returning with a phone in fresh plastic packaging, the kind that comes from that outside world, the one I've always imagined to be clean and clear. The shopkeeper held out the phone, but didn't give it to me.

You came all the way here to buy this? he asked.

I came here for work, I said, and stuck out my hand, demanding the phone in exchange for my answer.

He handed it over.

What job could be had here? he replied. His response was part statement and part question. Perhaps there was a business opportunity he'd overlooked.

I was in the Special Lashkar, I said, but left only recently because of an accident.

An accident? he asked.

An unfortunate one, I said. I've been to this village before, when I was a soldier. I need work and this seemed like a good place to start looking.

The strength of my story was that it was almost the whole truth. There was no reason to hide that I used to be a soldier, in fact this would make the news of my presence spread quickly, and hopefully to Atal.

With my story planted, I paid for my phone and left the store. On my way out from the bazaar, I stopped by one of the open-air stalls and bought a heavy blanket and a foam mattress. As I turned to leave, a woman in a pale blue burka edged next to me. I tensed my body, struggling not to stare at her. Slowly she looked over the blankets, pillows, pots and pans that were on display. She was covered and her head never turned in my direction, but from behind the mesh face screen of the burka, I felt her eyes hang on me. And I knew it was Fareeda.

She said nothing, she couldn't, but she stood next to me and lazily ran her good hand on the soft blankets. I wanted to pour myself out to her and take her all the way back through everything – Tawas, my brother, Commander Sabir, her uncle, badal. I wanted her to understand. But she couldn't and she couldn't speak with me, a stranger and a man, in public. Still she stood there. In the quiet and the standing was a sympathy. And as she turned to leave, the back of her hand touched mine and I felt I'd soon see Atal.

★

When I returned, Iskander was napping in the middle of the dirt courtyard. His belly was upturned to the sun and his paws were extended and bent at the wrist. I walked into the house where I found Mumtaz in a similar position next to the stove. He writhed on the floor, scratching his back against it, and I looked out the door and to the courtyard, where Iskander now did the same. Tucked in the corner of the room was Mumtaz's bedding. I placed my new blanket and pillow next to his. We had no wood. I'd burned it all. And the thought of spending the night in this room with Mumtaz was enough for me, I didn't want to spend the day with him too, so I took to the hills in search of firewood and a place where I could send a message to Commander Sabir unnoticed.

By late morning the streets were nearly empty. Packs of dirt-faced children kicked up dust, rough-housing and chasing the feral dogs who roamed in competing packs, but aside from this, the men had taken to whatever work they had and the women toiled inside their compounds. I could've left the village in any direction, but the eastern border loomed, drawing me to its snowcapped mountains and slopes covered with stubborn pines. I travelled a narrow path out of the village that weaved through an easy rise of foothills before it ran in switchbacks to the altitudes.

I hiked among the trees, stacking felled branches into small piles along the path, climbing ever higher. Soon I stood amid an

169

outcropping of grey rocks that broke through the thick forest. This was where Commander Sabir wanted to build the outpost. I understood why. The ground commanded the valley below. Among the rocks there was a large boulder held in place by several bent trunk pines that had grown, and now strained, at its base. This dangerous balance had likely existed longer than the village. From such a height, the mud-walled compounds and dirt lanes appeared like undiscovered mites in the flank of the mountain, protected only by their insignificance. I crouched between the boulder and the face and shielded myself from the gaze of anyone below. I took out my phone and punched in the numbers that tethered me to my other life, *09973285676*. Then I sent a single word: ARRIVED.

As I admired the view, I heard a crash beneath me. I crouched and strained to see between the trunks. The crash came again. Low voices followed. I sat motionless and exposed. To move would've been most dangerous of all.

Three men with a lean and hard appearance, but nearly frail, crossed the steep mountain on the sides of their feet. A youthful whine came from the back of the column: We should sleep at the flat rock, even if we used it two nights ago.

The youth had a fresh face and wore a black shalwar kameez under a red sequined vest. The vest was gaudy like those worn by circus monkeys, but any amusement I felt at his appearance left me when I saw the steel mortar tube balanced on his shoulder.

Don't get lazy, said the man in front.

His comments seemed at odds with his appearance as he stumbled forwards, holding his rifle by the barrel, nearly dragging it on the ground. The fighters sifted between the trees. Their clothes fit loosely, and it was only where a shoulder strap pressed, or a belt of ammunition was slung, that their hungry bodies could be seen. I imagined what was unseen. I thought these men were so starved that if I pressed their aching stomachs, my fingers might count out the bones on their spines. I wondered if they had any capacity to imagine another life. If they didn't, this was their greatest suffering.

Their footsteps faded across the ridgeline, but I squatted and strained to hear the complete silence that would assure me they'd passed. Soon the quiet of the mountains returned. I stood, slowly, and descended, gathering the firewood I'd left along the path. By the time I'd made it halfway down, I strained to see over the heap in my arms and stumbled towards the village.

Suddenly a pair of hollow thuds rang out from the direction the three men had departed in. A thin finger of smoke rose through the trees and quickly blew to nothing. For a moment, all drew silent again. Then, just outside the village, the earth sprouted skyward in two places. Still it was silent, until rushing towards me came the *crump* of the impacts as their noise spilled over the mountains.

I froze. From above the woodpile in my arms, I looked down into the village. There was nothing I could do. I was in no danger. I knew where the mortar team was and was glad I wasn't sitting with Mumtaz and Iskander below. The dust from the first two impacts cleared. The village offered little reaction, no people diving into their homes, no mothers running down the streets to protect their children. Everyone paused, looked up, and continued their business as though they'd noticed the first snowflakes on a day when the sky was already heavy and the air already cold.

Two more hollow thuds rang out. I awaited the second salvo with greater fear than I had the first. The crew would've adjusted their aim now and the impacts would be among the homes. The rounds hung in the air, but tore up the earth in the exact same place. No adjustments had been made. It seemed the mortar crew missed on purpose. As the *crump* tumbled along the mountainside, the villagers below paid less attention to this salvo than to the first. Children still taunted dogs in the streets and men still lazed in the open air of the bazaar.

Suddenly my phone vibrated. I laid down my woodpile and checked it. Commander Sabir had left a text: UNDERSTOOD. I crouched against the hillside and fumbled through the pop-up menus until I managed to delete the message and the incoming phone number. With that finished, I rushed down the mountainside towards Mumtaz's compound, confident that my armful of firewood would keep him happy and that gossip had already spread through the village – an old soldier from the Special Lashkar was looking for work.

I SPENT MOST OF MY TIME with Mumtaz, leaving his compound only to gather firewood or, on occasion, to wander down to the bazaar in the hope that someone might mention to Atal that I'd been there. Mumtaz and I spent a great deal of time sipping tea, petting Iskander – who eventually allowed me to scratch him behind his clipped ears – and sharing stories.

Mumtaz's enthusiasm for this last activity was unmatched. Each morning, as soon as I had loaded the stove with dry branches and stoked a good flame, I'd prop myself against my mattress and he'd begin. He told me of his family, stories that felt ancient, stories from before the war. He spoke of his father, who drove a truck, and how when he was a boy he'd accompanied him as far as Isfahan to the west, Lahore to the east, and Tashkent to the north. His father's business had been prosperous and when Mumtaz was younger, he'd dreamt of building it into something larger than the work of a single man. Also he told me of his brother and how they would steal eggs from chicken coops like the one Iskander slept in and trade them for cigarettes in the bazaar.

After each story Mumtaz would make an appeal: Aziz, you're

still a young man. Know these stories so we can remember a way that is different than now. The future is in the remembering.

I'd nod back patiently. With each urging my affection for the old man grew.

Mumtaz also had war stories. He told these with a deep solemnity and only after dinner, in that quiet space before sleep when great truths fall from our mouths like ripe fruit from wind-shaken branches. He spoke of the war's early days in Gomal, when educated and idealistic men fought the Russians.

We all had a future then, he said. We understood what it meant to sacrifice that small future for a bigger one. Such sacrifice is what it meant to be a mujahid and this is why all the mujahideen are now dead, even the living ones such as me are dead. Now the cause is war for advantage, war for profit, not a future.

But when he let go of the bitterness and told of the men he'd considered mujahideen, he spoke his words as if to rouse them from sleep and back to their youth. One night he crouched behind the stove as though laying in ambush behind a pine. He jumped forwards, his words rushing breathlessly through him: From inside the forest, my brother and I shot off the RPGs. Then we charged the Russians. The tanks burned and in moments their armoured column was nothing more than a string of charred metal and a mob of pale-faced boys crying for mercy, their cheeks stained by their blood and peach fuzz. We gave no quarter and that was just for we would've received none.

Mumtaz described in tall terms the gunships that were sent against his small band after the ambush. Two, he said excitedly, or was it three? No, it couldn't have been three, because they always flew in pairs, so it must have been four. Those fools couldn't find us. My brother and I hid the rest of the day near the border, behind a large boulder, where we'd often cache our weapons.

I wondered if this was the same boulder I'd used to hide my communication with Commander Sabir. It likely was. Little ever changed in a village or in a war like this. The best hiding spots and places for ambush were passed down like heirlooms.

When I awoke the morning after that story, Mumtaz was already up. He sat propped against the wall with Iskander spread across his lap. He alternated between tugging at his moustache and petting the burr-tangled coat on the dog's stomach. He stared towards the cold stove in the room's centre, blankly.

I fed branches for the morning's fire into the stove.

We're almost out of wood, I said. I'll gather some today.

But I needed to check my phone. It'd been nearly a week since I'd reported my arrival.

No need for that, replied Mumtaz still staring out towards nothing. Today it's too cold outside. I think tomorrow will be warm. Go then.

Fine, tomorrow, I said.

I lit our fire and sat next to him in silence. The room gathered its heat. With it, Mumtaz's frozen expression thawed. I haven't remembered my brother in a long time, he said. His end didn't come well. For him or for me, so the remembering is always difficult.

But you have many good memories of him, I answered, and thought of Ali, and all I would do so his end might not yet be a memory.

I do, he said. But, over the years, I've lost him in his end.

The two of us sat silently for a time. Our fire crackled down to embers and I crossed the room to fill the stove again. My movement jarred something in Mumtaz and he spoke, not to me but to an empty space, his unstable voice trying to land on something solid.

When my brother died, he said, it was not in the war we thought we fought. We were mujahideen and treated as heroes in this village, our battlefield achievements known by all, earning us honour, honour we became greedy for. This led to larger and more daring attacks. When the fighting slowed each winter, we'd grow impatient for it. The Russians stayed on their bases and it was difficult to strike at them. An informant of ours in Orgun, a man who like our father ran a trucking company, told us how in a few nights a Russian convoy would pass our village along the north road. Eager as we were, my brother and I asked few questions. The operation would be simple. After curfew we'd bury a mine in the road and in the morning, if the Russians didn't show up, we'd remove it.

Some days later, in the darkness, my brother and I chipped a ditch out of the frozen earth and slid the mine in. We carefully repacked the crumbled soil and went home, giving the matter little thought, as if we'd planted a tree and casually wondered if it'd grow. We slept soundly and early the following morning, before the sun rose, we returned to either inspect our kill or to recover the mine. As we walked through the clear cold air, the snow on the distant hilltops glowed with firelight. The mine had struck and we approached the road riding on great gusts of enthusiasm. But still, our situation was uncertain. Who knew if the Russians had sent anyone to aid their convoy? Who knew if we'd come across any manic survivors? These were uncertainties we felt prepared for. We weren't prepared for what we found. As we crested a last ridge and glimpsed our kill, we saw only the beginning of our terrible mistake.

Tilted against its side as if the carcass of a great steel beast was the truck, but it wasn't Russian. It was civilian and full of lumber that now burned in a pyre, sparkling on the snow. We kept our distance but were close enough to feel the fire on our faces. We could see the cab and its white paint, which curled to scales against the heat, and then the steel beneath the paint that scorched to rust. Behind a shattered windshield, flames licked out of an upright silhouette that burned with the dignity of one who met death immediately, without pain and shock, and through this absence seemed strangely alive. I can't say how long we watched the pyre. When we left, the sun still hadn't risen but the silhouette had been consumed. On our journey home, we said nothing and tried to hide in our silence.

News of the attack spread through all the families of Gomal. The truck had been from our informant's company and the dead driver had been his employee. Several days later, my father and our village's spingaris were called to a jirga in Orgun to settle the matter. The deliberations were short, lasting but two days, and my father returned in ruin. The spingaris on both sides decreed that our father was responsible for our actions and that he must replace the destroyed truck and buy yet another to recoup the damaged cargo. In this our informant made out very well, for the first truck forced us to sell our home and the second wiped out my father's accounts, eliminating him as a business competitor. That's when we moved here.

Mumtaz waved his hands around the room and spat on his own floor. He put his finger in my face. That was not the worst of it, he said. The family of the driver was at the jirga. Instead of taking money for their son's death, money my father no longer had, they chose badal against my brother, the eldest son, a life for a life. This broke my father. To honour Pashtunwali, the family hired a qatal to hunt down my brother. Now he would have to live on the run.

The day after my father returned, I stood with my brother in the morning's dark cold and wished him goodbye. He didn't tell my father he was going. He knew that the old man would do the honourable thing and try to protect him, so my brother did the honourable thing and left. Before he walked out of our gate, I grabbed his arm and, full of a younger brother's purpose, told him: That crook in Orgun will pay for what he's done. We will have badal, and the truth will be known, and you will return.

My brother grabbed the back of my neck and pulled me close to him. The fourteen months between us always gave him a slit of insight I was yet to have, but now that slit split to a chasm. He looked at me and spoke as if from its other side: Your badal is to take none. Break that chain. Leave the war. Care for Father.

I protested, but he turned and walked away from our house and our village and south into the mountains whose ridges received him like the fingers of an outstretched hand.

I did as my brother asked. I cared for our father. I made him comfortable in this room and we tried to continue our life. Without the business we slipped into poverty, but my brother was alive and our imagined reunion kept us from the truest form of poverty, despair. But several months later, a visitor delivered that despair. The man arrived at our gate so early in the morning that he must have travelled through the night. He was a tall man, and skinny but for a pair of powerful hands. On one wrist he wore a digital watch. It was gold and hung loosely like a bracelet. On its screen, I saw the time. His watch ran eight hours fast, as if he'd reset the days, making our early morning his afternoon. Over his clothing, he wore a blue vest embroidered in gold braid and the running end of his turban dangled over its front. The

178

turban was yellow, nearly matching the gold braid of his vest. It perched on his head, piled into a mound. Standing in the dust of our modest home, his elegance was nearly obscene.

We invited him to come inside, sit, and have tea with us, but he held up his palm, refusing. I don't ask for hospitality, he said, only that you hear my message, which will free me of my duty. My father nodded and the man continued: A week ago your son was killed. The badal was sanctioned by the Orgun jirga of two months past. Your son is buried in the communal graves outside the Blue Mosque in Spin Boldak. If you go there and ask for the undertaker, he can help you arrange the body's transport here. These are directions to the grave.

The man offered my father, who couldn't read, a piece of paper the size of a banknote. My father's hand shook as he took the paper.

And how is it that you have such knowledge of my son? he asked.

Badal is my duty, said the man. It is just that you be told of your son's end.

My father ran his eyes over the man and his beautiful clothes, knowing that in front of him stood his son's killer. Honourable men, he said, seem to be well compensated in matters of duty.

The qatal smiled, his lips rolling back to reveal gums that were pocked white as if with a coming sickness. Then he turned and left. My father clutched the note to his chest and he went back in the house where he lay down on his sleeping mat and pulled his blanket over his tiny shoulders. We had no money to go to Spin Boldak and never would. My brother is still buried there.

Mumtaz looked towards the ceiling, his eyes glossed with wetness. Still he spoke: My father died some weeks after that. I've been alone since. This was all a long time ago. So when I tell you my brother was killed in the war, you understand me.

He was killed in the war that is always among us and sustains so many with its profits. His last wish for me was to escape that war and I have. There may be little to admire in my life. I am a poor man without a family, but the war has no hold on me.

I patted Mumtaz's shoulder and told him: You are not so poor, old man. You have me to gather your firewood and I'll be paying you a week's rent for food and lodging.

Mumtaz rested his hand heavily on mine. He leaned back and took in my face with glassy eyes that hinted at both his grief and his age. He twirled the ends of his moustache to points and nodded. Tomorrow, he said, you'll gather some more wood for us, but keep your money. You are right. I am not so poor as some.

*

The next morning, I rose well before dawn and hurried towards the mountains. I had told Mumtaz I'd gather us some more wood, but what I really needed to do was send Commander Sabir a report, but, having made no progress contacting Atal, I dreaded doing so. I climbed the footpath quickly. Once I reached the high forest, I strained to see between the trunks and find the large boulder I'd hidden behind before. Then, after nearly an hour of searching, the grey rock face suddenly stood unmistakable in the distance.

I ran off the path and dried pine needles crushed and bounced beneath my feet. I arrived at the boulder's base and pulled out my cell phone. Its green light flashed in the darkness with a message. Beneath me, the rising sun swept the night shadow across the valley floor. I opened the phone. Its screen shone brightly and I worried I might be seen. My instincts told me to put it away, but I needed to send an update to Commander Sabir.

He'd already sent me a single word: STATUS?

Each imagined response seemed inadequate. What had I done? I'd sat with Mumtaz and waited. My status? My status was waiting, and that was not a message I could send back. Why hadn't Atal found me? I assumed Fareeda would tell him I was in the village. Perhaps I'd assumed too much.

Wedged between the boulder and the mountainside, I felt squeezed. Thirsting for the open air, I climbed the granite face of the boulder. I lay on my stomach with my head in profile and looked towards the valley and the village below. Soon the sun became full and its rays dodged through the clouds, landing many pieces of light against the earth, as if a broken jigsaw had spilled across the ground. In Gomal, tin-can chimneys pushed through the sinew of thatched roofs and smoke billowed as if the valley floor were the smattered embers of a single fire.

A long column of smoke poured from Mumtaz's chimney and I thought of the old man using the last of our firewood to push the morning chill from his mud room. I felt affection for him and admired how, by refusing to side with anyone, he defied the many deceptions swirling about him. Commander Sabir, Gazan, Atal, me, he defied us all, sat in his house, and warded off the cold with a few scraps of wood and a feral dog with clipped ears.

But one home in the valley called me to act. It was rubbled in parts with a white HiLux in front. Atal was brazen to park it there. After the raid at the madrassa, I couldn't show my face among the Special Lashkar for fear and shame, but Atal still drove around in the same truck.

I came up from my stomach and stood on the boulder. From this perch, I towered over Atal's home as though I could jump down and stamp it beneath my feet. Atal wouldn't find me as I'd hoped. There could be no more waiting. Action was mine to take. I pulled out my phone. STATUS? The question was an affront, and I sent Commander Sabir my response: CONTACT MADE.

I climbed off the boulder, bounded down the mountainside, and set out to make contact the only way I knew how, by knocking on Atal's front door. Mumtaz would have to wait.

★

I stood next to Atal's HiLux. Aside from Haji Jan's death, the damage from last month's mortar attack was slight. Two sides of the compound's outer wall had been destroyed as well as a small shed that held a generator, but the main house remained. From the rubbled gap in the wall, I could see the generator. It sat inert in the shed like a fat man collapsed from a heart attack, everything intact but lifeless. The red gate Mortaza and I came to on our first visit was also undamaged. Though I could've entered the compound through the broken cinder blocks of the old wall, I knocked and waited. I could see Atal cross the courtyard through the gap but pretended I couldn't, lest he feel shame for his crumbling home.

I wondered how long you'd wait with that old man, he said, throwing open the gate's steel latch. Before I could reply, he turned and walked towards the main house. I followed close behind. The air around him seemed heavy and stale. The scent of his perfume was missing.

Inside we entered the room where he'd entertained me before, when I was a soldier. We sat across from one another on plush leather sofas that could've seated nearly fifteen in better times. In the room's centre was an empty glass table.

Atal called to the back of the house: Fareeda, we have a guest!

The girl floated between rooms, her steps quick and small, as she prepared whatever hospitality would be given.

Atal said nothing. He wouldn't be the first to speak. Instead, he offered me an uncomfortable stare that questioned why I'd sought him out.

I'm looking for work, I said.

Atal had on the same powder-blue shalwar kameez and gold turban he'd worn the first time we'd met, but the hem of both were now soiled with grime. The gold turban's running end draped over his shoulder and down his front. He picked at a stain on its edge with his thumbnail and spoke without looking up: You killed a man, yes?

I nodded.

I heard this, he said. You killed a man at the madrassa when you tried to kill me. Atal shook his head and spoke softly, asking: Sabir fired you for this?

The man I killed had a brother in the Special Lashkar, I answered. His badal wouldn't allow me to stay.

I see, he said. So what is it you want?

You're being hunted, I told him. I don't know or understand why, but you are. You need help.

Atal shrugged. Hanging from his neck was the opal on the silver chain. He rolled it between his index finger and thumb and gazed around his plush but diminished room. Since his generator had died, he'd bought a wood-burning stove. There was no electric light in his house, and a paleness dusted the sofas, table, and Hitachi with its flat but empty screen.

And who says you're not my hunter? he asked.

There is a blood feud against me, I explained. I'm a dead man in the Special Lashkar. I need to make a new livelihood, that's why I'm here. And you, you need help.

Fareeda entered, balancing a plain silver platter between her good arm and body. Stacked on it was a teakettle and a dish half full of pine nuts. She rested it along the glass table.

Atal's phone rang. He pulled it from the pocket of his shalwar kameez and his face livened when he saw the number. Excuse me, he said, and rushed into the courtyard.

Fareeda and I were alone. She set small silver plates across the table. Her eyes were downcast but purposeful as she worked. Then, without looking up, she spoke: I've seen you in a dream.

A dream? I asked.

Yes, she said. I've seen you in one.

You are a part of this dream? I replied.

Sometimes, she said. The dream is always the same, but whether or not I am part of it is all that changes.

What is the dream? I asked.

In it, she began, I watch you from above and you are walking through the mountains and the pines. At first, I can't see where you are going, only that you are travelling upward and in a very straight way. You start in the low ground and you struggle against the rocks and the dirt. Soon you reach the high mountains, where there is snow, and as you step on it, it crunches very loudly under your feet and I am worried that you make too much noise. The higher you climb, the louder you become. Soon you are pulling against branches and their snow is falling on you and you are no longer walking straight, but thrashing in circles.

Then what happens? I said.

It depends, she answered, and looked at me with great care. Sometimes you tear through the mountains and disappear into them. I strain to see you but I can't. You are swallowed by the trees and the snow.

184

And other times? I asked.

Other times, I come down from above and I see your face and cheeks, and your hair tips dusted with the snow, and I stand next to you in the trees. But when you see me, I am not as I am now.

Fareeda looked down at her arm and then continued: And seeing my change, you are calmed and we walk together saying nothing.

This is a good dream, I said.

She untied her hijab and smoothed down her hair.

Sometimes it is, she replied. And now that you've found my uncle, what will you do?

He is in a difficult position. I can help.

She looked back, upset, as though my help were a lie, or as though she knew the difficulty of his position to be the truth.

Why does he need you? she asked.

I know and understand those who would harm him. Then I spoke more firmly: I can help.

And why would you do this?

I too need to survive, I said. You care for your uncle and he cares for you. If I help him, maybe he will help me.

Those who become too much involved with others destroy themselves by it, she said.

Perhaps this will be different, I replied.

Nothing is ever different.

And as she said it, I felt the great pain she carried. I reached towards her, slowly, lifting the shawl that hung over her knotted arm. She didn't move away and she didn't look at me, and, as I touched the one arm, I could feel how her soft skin covered the hard flesh beneath, consuming her. Her eyes met mine, but I saw no love in them, they held only that mix of beauty and indifference that is in all nature. My love and appreciation of her beauty meant no more to her than did all of man's to the forests and mountains that command us. I felt that indifference. It hurt and it is also what made her truly beautiful.

But still she stood, and I sat, and we shared our space for a long moment. Then Atal returned, and before he saw us, I let go of her.

His face was rutted by thought. He took a handful of pine nuts off the tray and spoke to Fareeda: Thank you, Gul, Flower.

She nodded, looked at me, and slipped into the back of the house.

Atal followed her with his gaze and only spoke once she was out of sight: I have a task for you, Aziz. If you perform it, we'll go from there, agreed?

What is the task? I asked.

There is a man coming to see me tomorrow night, explained Atal. He, like you, is one I'm learning to trust. He plans to meet me on the footpath that runs towards the border, do you know it?

I do.

Good, he said. If you want to protect me, find him on the path. You will then call back here and I'll give you further instructions. Once this is done, we'll talk more about our work together.

And who should I tell him I am?

Just tell him you're my friend, said Atal. He's a simple man and shouldn't give you any problems.

Write down your number for me, I said.

I would prefer you memorise it, he replied.

I nodded.

09973284643, he told me. Shall I say it again?

I shook my head.

You are certain? he asked.

186

09973284643, I answered.

He nodded.

Numbers are easy, I said.

*

I left Atal's compound and returned to the high forest. I finished collecting wood for Mumtaz. I gathered branches along the same footpath that I'd travel the next night. As I did, the footpath cut through the trees like a scar I'd soon share with the mountains. If the man was so simple, why was Atal afraid to meet him alone? I wandered off the path and gathered more dry branches in the shade. My mind drifted to months earlier, when I'd first met Atal in the village, and how he now seemed worn down by violence and responsibility. I imagined him running out the madrassa's back door on the night I killed Tawas and as I recalled that miserable part of my past, I understood his, and remembered the binjo parked next to his truck, and if I hadn't known before, I knew now. The simple man I'd meet would be Gazan.

I FINISHED MY WORK along the footpath and staggered out of the mountains, towards Mumtaz's home, my arms filled with enough firewood to last several days. Gusts of wind blew down the narrow lanes of Gomal, whipping up swirls of dust that dissolved into a powdery haze. Looking over my bundle, I saw one of the grocers from the bazaar standing at Mumtaz's gate. Against his ankle leaned a bag of rice. He bent his thin frame forwards as he pointed a snuff-stained fingernail in Mumtaz's face.

If I give it to you for seven hundred, I make no profit, said the grocer.

You gave it to me two weeks ago for seven hundred, said Mumtaz.

That was two weeks ago, replied the grocer. As long as the roads stay closed the cost of everything goes up. Now it is seven hundred fifty. In two more weeks likely eight hundred, and then, who can say?

Mumtaz shook his head. He seemed both amazed at the rise in prices and indignant that Gazan, Atal, and Commander Sabir could hold an entire village's economy hostage.

Ah, Mumtaz, here comes your young friend, the old soldier, said the grocer as I approached. Perhaps he knows when a bag of rice won't cost a month's pay.

I set my pile of wood next to Mumtaz and told him: I'll get more once we use this. Then I bowed gently, showing him, as my host, the fullest respect I could. I said nothing to the grocer, but reached into my pocket and peeled three notes from the roll of money I'd left the Special Lashkar with. I pressed them into his hand.

Enough? I asked him.

The grocer gave a sly grin and slid the notes into his pocket without counting them. Then he reached into his mouth and hooked out a piece of snuff from under his lower lip. It sat dripping on his finger, green and furry as a caterpillar. He flung it at my feet and it crumbled in the dirt.

For a traveller looking for work, you have a great deal of money, he said.

I have work, I replied. I work for Atal and he works for this village.

I grabbed the bag of rice that leaned against the grocer's ankle. I tossed it into the courtyard. Then I picked up the firewood and walked inside.

Mumtaz returned to the one room we shared as I stacked the firewood in the corner. So you've found your job? he asked, his voice quiet.

I nodded.

You've taken sides with Atal then.

I've chosen only to survive.

Mumtaz picked a handful of branches off the pile I'd stacked. He filled the stove with them, struck a match, and touched its flame to their ends. The dry wood cracked louder and louder as its heat spread. He left the stove's door open so the air could feed into it.

Atal through his meddling has made even survival a side, he said.

He shut the door to the stove. The room warmed. He was right. I had taken a side, my second.

★

The next evening Mumtaz and I each ate a full plate of rice. Once we'd finished, he took the last scraps of our meal to the chicken coop and fed them to Iskander. The old man figured that whatever work I did for Atal was night work, and he didn't want to hear my lies as I left to do it.

From Mumtaz's house, I walked quickly through the lanes of the village. They spilled out to the low open hills, which fed up into the forested mountains. The sun had just set by the time I reached the nearest of the pines. Behind me, day still glowed on the open ground. To my front the footpath ran into the shaded tree rows where night had already taken hold. Somewhere in that dark and sloping forest was Gazan.

The dirt path cut its way upward like a black ribbon, tracing the rise and fall of the mountain. At times, when darkness flooded the forest completely, I lost the path and only found it again by feeling for its loose dirt with my feet. Hours passed and my quick steps yielded to an exhausted march as I rose into the emptier air. Fear laid its grip on me. Would I accidentally follow the path too far and cross the border, or would I stop too short and miss my meeting? I buried my fists in my pockets, squeezing fear into the phone I clutched with my right hand and the fold of cash I clutched with my left. The night chilled as I climbed higher and cool traces of sweat beaded on my back. Suddenly, I rose from the dark forest and into a bare field along the highest ridge-top. Here patches of snow reflected the moonlight. I stood, exposed and afraid. I'd walked as far as I dared, finding no one.

I waited in the high snows long enough to feel my warm body turn cold, forcing me down from the summit. Travelling in reverse, my path twisted before me like something entirely new. I moved faster, and as the bald ridgetop blended into the forest's shadow below, I felt a fresh commitment to find Gazan among the wilderness.

I entered the pine rows and walked slowly, my whole body straining as I gazed between the trunks, eager to discover him, instead of him, me. Then a warm hand grabbed my shoulder. A whisper: Am I what you've searched this whole path for?

Though he was a grown man, his body was meagre as a boy's. He seemed like one of those old trees in the forest that through lack of light and rain never rise taller than saplings. His hair grew into a thick beard that came to a point, sweeping to one side like a worn broom does. The beard was dark too, so dark it matched the path we stood on. He smiled widely. His grin reflected the moonlight just as the snow had been reflected atop the ridgeline. A bolt-action Lee-Enfield hung lazily from his shoulder and his clothing hung lazily from his body. A great uncertainty overtook me. I struggled to speak.

The man pumped his arm twice above his head, and nearly a dozen figures stepped silently from amid the trees. They formed a forest inside the forest and I stood among them.

There is someone I'm supposed to meet here, but you are not him, said the man, his tone friendly and yet sinister. He leaned closer to my face and considered it.

I work for Atal, I said.

The man nodded, looking at the cold steady figures that surrounded us. That is who I am supposed to meet, he said, but you are not him.

He sent me to find you, I answered.

And what were you to do when you found me? he asked.

I pulled the phone from my pocket. The man stepped back with a start, dipping his shoulder, unslinging his ancient rifle.

He told me to call when I found you! I spoke quickly.

The man pointed his rifle away from me, and to the ground. He grabbed a palmful of his beard and twirled its end around his index finger. Make your call, he said, but I wish to speak with him.

I slowly opened my phone and its screen glowed, blinding us and making the night darker. I punched in Atal's number and got a pre-recorded message from Roshan, the phone company, in what sounded like Urdu. I tried again with the same result. I felt the gunmen and the forest close in on me as I struggled to complete the call. Had I forgotten the number? I could still hear myself reciting it back to Atal.

It'll be morning at the rate you're going, said the man. Your boss should be in there.

He tossed me his phone. I opened it, pushed the send key, and scanned the recent call list for Atal's number, *09973284643*. It was on top. I'd been correct, the shopkeeper must have sold me a bad SIM card. Relief surged down my body and then I saw another number listed below, *09973285676*. My relief cut to numbness as sure as if my spine had been severed. It was Commander Sabir's number, the one that should only be memorised, never saved to a phone, the one that was a secret. Why was it there? From the mobile's screen, a deceit I didn't yet understand shined back at me, its luminous halo beaming upward from my hands, *09973285676*.

With guns trained on me in the darkness, I called the first number. Atal answered immediately: Gazan, I sent a man to find you, has he? The second truth of the night – *Gazan*. I'd convinced myself the man I'd meet would be him, but Atal confirmed it. It was real. Badal confronted me. I knew I wanted to kill him, but I didn't feel the want. I felt nothing, nothing but the little numbing. I willed myself to hate him. I thought of the photo Taqbir had given me, and Ali's desperate look into a place I'd never seen and from which I could never recover him. Still, there was only the numbness. All I felt was *09973285676*. Those digits had once been a prayer of certainty and now, from them, everything fell into confusion.

No, this is Aziz, I answered quickly. I am with him now.

I handed the phone to Gazan, whose eyes sat wide, off-white, and satisfied above cheekbones that ran across his face sharp as knives. He enjoyed the power he held at our introduction. Gazan and Atal spoke in muted tones, and I looked away as though it were my eyes that heard.

First you insult me by sending your chai boy and now you ask that I walk into your home alone and with no assurances, said Gazan.

I strained to overhear Atal's response but couldn't.

And what is he to me? asked Gazan. We agreed to meet on the path.

Atal said something else I couldn't understand.

That may be so, replied Gazan, but you've broken faith. Why should I trust you with something more, with my life no less?

Gazan sneered and looked at me from slitted eyes as he listened to Atal. He then relaxed and began to nod in agreement.

Yes, he said, if that is your offer, it is a fair assurance. With that I'll come.

Gazan slid the phone into his pocket.

You're staying here, he told me.

He waved two men over who had been hovering behind me. One of them stepped around my side. Set across his broad and worn face was a dark grey beard, hanging to his chest. He tipped his wide-panned Waziri pakol at me in a sort of apology that we should meet as captor and captive.

Watch him until I return, said Gazan. If I'm not back by sunrise, kill him.

He went casually down the footpath towards Atal's home. I remained a hostage in a negotiation I didn't understand.

As soon as Gazan was out of sight, the older man in the pakol nodded towards the forest. Follow him, please, he said.

Another man stepped from behind me. Draped across his lean, raw-boned shoulders was the smooth steel of a mortar tube and a green canvas rucksack that sank heavily down his back. A red vest with elaborate sequins added to his delicate features and did nothing to make him appear more fearsome. This was the youth I'd seen walking through the woods before the mortar attack weeks ago. The recognition of something, even something sinisterly familiar, calmed me. Both of us were about the same age, for I was also just recently a man.

These two sandwiched me between them, leading me off the footpath, along the floor of soft needles, and deeper into a blanket of pine that rolled across the ridgeline. The forest grew cooler and cooler as we wandered to its depths. Like the bottom of a lake, the trees trapped a cold reminder that the sun struggles to touch all parts of the earth equally. As we walked, I felt that peculiar itch in my spine, which is the possibility of a bullet in the back. The rest of Gazan's fighters travelled in a loose unseen ring about us. None spoke. With each step farther from the footpath, I wondered whether Gazan would manage to find his way back to us, and if he didn't, whether I would receive a polite bullet at sunrise from my friend, the older man with the pakol.

Eventually the youth in the red vest stopped and sat. I had no idea where we were, but I felt grateful that we were no longer moving. I too sat and the forest was quiet. I strained to see in the night but couldn't separate the fighters from the surrounding pines. In the altitude, my body cooled. Next to me metal scraped on metal. The youth worked at the base of his mortar. He raised his head towards me. Come here! he shouted in a whisper.

I slid on my side towards him, cautiously, as though we sat on the roof of some great house. Hold this up, he demanded. Slowly, I came to my knees and helped him balance the mortar. He examined the bottom of the tube as though he were blowing against a dying fire. He twisted and tugged at the base and again metal scraped on metal. Whatever he did, he did by touch alone, never fouling the darkness with a light, and this discipline seemed contrary to his sequined red vest.

The older man stood above us. Did you put it in? he asked.

The youth sat up. He wiped his hands against his black shalwar kameez. It's in, he said, but if we break another firing pin this mortar will be useless.

Does Gazan know that's the last one? asked the older man.

He knows, said the youth. The question is, do his friends know, and will they give us more. In his voice I heard cynicism and weariness.

The older man squatted next to me. How did you come into the service of a man like Atal? he asked.

I used to be a soldier in the Special Lashkar, I said.

The older man tugged at his greying beard. Just like that? he asked.

Just like what? I replied.

You go from strangling Gomal and chasing us through the mountains to working for a man such as Atal, he said. Just like that, eh?

A man like Atal, I answered. What type of man do you mean?

Now the youth spoke: Atal is the type of fool who'd try to teach a dog to drink cream or a cat to chew a bone.

You ask why I work for Atal? It is my livelihood, I said. Commander Sabir provided my livelihood, now Atal does.

The old man spoke again: Yes, we all work in the same way. Atal will pay Gazan for meeting him tonight and Commander Sabir will give us money to continue our mortar attacks against Gomal. But I remember when there were other ways to have a livelihood. There were other things. How we did them, I can't say, it was so long ago. I remember only that we did.

The youth took off his green rucksack. In the dark, he clumsily tugged against the buckles on the top flap, unfastening them. Next, he carefully reached into the main pouch as though he were taking a dish from the oven. He pulled out an anti-tank mine cased in green plastic and about the size of a hubcap. He rested it upside down on the rucksack. Then he twisted a plastic switch on its bottom until there was a noise like a pencil breaking. The corners of his lips crept into a grin. He put the mine back into his rucksack. For your old friends on the north road, the morning will come hard and early, he said.

His excitement unsettled me.

Must you enjoy it so? muttered the older man.

And why shouldn't I? asked the youth.

No reason, he said.

The three of us sat in silence. The pine needles beneath me became soggy with dew. Soon the first seam of blue appeared along a distant ridgeline and with it the noise of Gazan's footsteps shuffling tiredly towards us. The youth stood, his red vest a beacon for his commander. Gazan's eyes fixed on us through the trees. He stopped and waved his arm back towards the footpath. The rest of his fighters followed. The older man and the youth picked up their weapons and left me sitting on the pine needles unguarded and alone. Nothing needed to be said. Gazan was back and I was free to go. Had he returned to his fighters an hour later, or not at all, they knew what to do with me. And had they done it, nothing would've been said either.

The fighters withdrew like a mist and I strained to see their movements as they sifted through the trees. Quickly! Gazan called after them. I've made assurances that the north road will be ready.

*

Early light etched hard edges into the shadows made by the pines. Through the forest I stared after Gazan and his men but saw and heard nothing. The silence unsettled me. I sprang to my feet and ran down the mountainside, towards Atal's home, dodging the trees.

Commander Sabir supported Gazan's attacks?

Why did Atal meet with Gazan?

Why was I sent to report on Atal?

How could I prevent the attack against my friends on the north road?

This last question stopped me. I pulled out my phone and typed a message to Commander Sabir: MINE PLANTED – NORTH

ROAD. It felt useless as a smoke signal, but there was nothing else I could do. I was wrapped in something artificial, something not understood. I was unsure to what end my message would come. I pressed Send, satisfying my duty to warn.

I continued to run, my sense of speed increasing as the sun rose. The steam from my sweating body lifted into the crisp air as I came from the woods and stood on the outskirts of the village. Smoke also lifted from Atal's chimney. The cooking fire inside had likely burned all through the night. I walked towards his home and what I hoped would be answers.

The front door was cracked open, either in expectation of my arrival or because of a careless guest's departure. I shut it behind me. Atal sat rigidly on the edge of his plush leather sofa. His stare was fixed on the wall, as though he were solving a math problem. Across from him, along the glass table, sat a half-eaten piece of naan and an empty cup of tea. I perched myself on the opposite sofa, interrupting his thoughts, but saying nothing. I waited for him to speak.

It is a careful thing I've enlisted you to do with me.

Tonight it felt reckless, I said.

Yes, but you must understand why I couldn't risk going up there. You are reliable. Those men are not.

Is this the work I'm to do? To play hostage for your meetings?

Tonight was necessary, forgive me, he said. But as I go further, I need a man who can help with my security.

What are we going further into?

Atal held his gaze on mine, affirming a decision in me that he'd already made. I am helping Gazan broker a peace with the Americans, he said.

He wants peace? I replied, my voice thick with doubt.

He swears it.

Why? And if you're concerned about dealing with him, why don't you get the Americans to help with your security?

Before I could say anything else, Atal raised his palm.

I think you misunderstand, he said. The threat to my security isn't Gazan. He is manageable. It is Sabir. Sabir keeps Gazan's fighters equipped. Sabir pays them to mortar Gomal so the spingaris might bend to his will. And Sabir makes sure that a steady stream of youths, like you, join his ranks searching for badal against men who did them harm in a war that he fuels. The threat is Sabir.

My mind raced. Commander Sabir's number had been in Gazan's cell phone, suggesting what Atal divulged. His revelations confirmed my worst fears. It is more difficult to unlearn than to learn, but Atal challenged me to understand this war's true nature, that it had no sides. Each was the same as another.

Gazan's men are as full of hate as any, I said. Why does he want peace?

Some of them are, he answered. But most are tired. They fight only for the livelihood the war provides. Gazan is tired. The only ones who are powerful enough to pluck him from his arrangement with Sabir are the Americans.

I leaned close to Atal and for the first time spoke to him as an equal might: Just like that, you would forgive Gazan? He dropped mortars on your home. He killed Haji Jan. He nearly killed you. You would let that go?

Atal's jaw clenched. He stroked the running end of his turban, starting at his shoulder. His tendons ran taut as steel wires beneath his olive skin, but by the time his hand travelled to the hem's bottom, it had relaxed. I've let nothing go, he said softly. Gazan and Sabir have taken more from me than this.

He stood. On the table in front of us sat a dented steel pot filled with now cold tea. He crossed the room and placed the pot atop his squat tin stove, much like the one in Mumtaz's home but newer. He opened its front and filled its belly with dry branches, just skinny enough for him to break in two. He cracked the wood between his hands and looked over his shoulder at me.

Stay, he said. I will prepare us some breakfast.

Atal lit a match and touched it gently to the ends of a leafy branch. The flame took slowly. Then, all at once, it spread as the dry leaves caught fire. He threw the branch in the stove. I hadn't noticed that the room was cold until it filled with quick warmth.

Atal sat on his haunches and faced the stove. Badal, he said, should resolve an injustice, not continue it. But that is our way. Some injustice is done against a man, so he continues it against others. That is the way of Commander Sabir. He learned this after what happened to his brother, Jazeem.

Did you know Jazeem? I asked.

No, he said, but there are few men whose fates have been tied closer to mine. The man who led the ambush that killed Jazeem, Hafez, was my cousin, not by blood but by friendship. Hafez had no real family. As boys we played in the same dirty alleys and sometimes lived in the same house, him sleeping on my family's floor in the winter. When I became a man, I inherited that house and a plot of land, not much, but a livelihood. Hafez had none of this. Soon he took to the mountains and found his livelihood in the war, fighting. I saw him from time to time when he would come out of the mountains. Only when Sabir gunned him down did I realise my obligation to him as family. I awoke that morning and Hafez's body was sprawled outside this house, delivered to me as his only kin. He lay there, legs straight out, head bent back on the wall, eyes rolled up, the whites peeking through slits. I still see it clearly.

We buried him. Then the entire village looked to me for badal. People who barely knew Hafez spoke to me of Pashtunwali, of right and wrong. He led the ambush against Jazeem, but he did not kill him! they'd say. Others told me: If Sabir was to take Hafez's life, he should have taken it in battle. That is fair, an assassination is not! They came to me with plenty of reasons and their reasons always ended with: There must be badal!

Hafez had gone to fight when he was angry and young. By the end, though, he'd forgotten his anger. In the months before he died, he'd come to my home every few weeks, delivering money to me. He asked that I give it to a woman who lived in Orgun, no questions. And in friendship that's what I did. But in the end whatever Hafez had found and built with this woman mattered little. Although he forgot the anger that first sent him to the mountains, it never forgot him. It took him

The kettle atop the stove came to a boil. Atal wrapped a towel around its handle and brought it to the table. He poured out two steaming cups and continued: For weeks after his death, I couldn't see the right path. To purpose myself towards killing Sabir seemed the only option that offered nang, but it would continue the same cycle that destroyed my cousin. One night my answer came as I slept. A noise woke me in this room. I walked out, rifle in hand. I imagined that Sabir or one of his men had come to kill me. In that moment I felt certain I'd acted too slowly, my foolish restraint was now my undoing. As I moved through my house, a desire for violence ran through me. I was determined to destroy whatever I found. And as I crept into this room, on that couch, where you sit, was a little girl, Fareeda. Her eyes were wet and wide with fear. When she saw me she began to sob. I set down my rifle, sat next to her, and she wept through her black hair into my shoulder. She was healthy then. Not as she is now.

Atal glanced down at his arm, but smiled as he thought of her in those days.

Fareeda is Hafez's daughter? I asked.

Who is to say? said Atal. At first she was gripped by silence and tears, but she came to tell me how her mother had paid a man to bring her to my house from Orgun. A few days later, I drove with her to the house where before I'd delivered Hafez's money. When I knocked on the door, a man I'd never seen answered. His face was scarred from pox and red as side meat. This was the type of person your eyes knew to avoid. At his appearance, Fareeda clung to my leg. It was the first time she'd embraced me. The man said that the woman who'd lived there before had been very poor and that he'd let her stay without rent for some months. He assured me of his kindness and virtue towards her and because of that was surprised when she'd suddenly left. But the man's dirty clothes and sickly appearance did not bespeak generosity. The world hadn't been generous to him, so what could be expected. But he looked at the little girl and promised he had done nothing to harm them.

By the time we travelled back from Orgun, I made a vow to keep Fareeda until her mother returned. Weeks passed and it became clear no one was coming. She'd been abandoned, and shortly after the disease took form in her arm. I then decided I had a niece and that Hafez's memory would be one of family. I committed my life to Fareeda out of respect for his memory.

From time to time, Sabir came to our village. He always paid me a visit or offered polite taunts in the shura. He'd tell the spingaris: Atal knows better than most the problems this village faces. Or he'd say: You above all understand why a family should not oppose the Special Lashkar. He hoped that I'd purpose my badal against him and in turn give him a purpose against me.

Atal sipped his tea and stroked his greying beard.

And Gazan? I asked.

Gazan was inevitable, said Atal. His reason for fighting I don't know. I imagine his tragedy is common. There will always be angry men ready to kill each other. But now Gazan swears he is for peace, and if I can help him find it through the Americans, I will. Peace with Gazan could break the cycle of fighting and this threatens all Sabir has. Tomorrow I am going to see my American contact in Shkin. I need your help to get there and back safely.

I sipped my tea, twisting my expression from uncertainty to resolve. I felt unsettled but told him: Of course I'll help.

Good. When Gazan left, said Atal, he warned me to stay off the north road today.

His men took a mine there, I replied. An attack against the Special Lashkar, it seems.

Yes, he said, I figured the same. It is a strange thing that Sabir lets his own dog bite him. We'll go tomorrow night then.

I nodded and swallowed the last of my tea.

At that moment we heard a sharp and faraway rumble. We rose and walked into Atal's courtyard. Outside, villagers stood on their rooftops and gawked into the distance. We gazed northward through a gap in the rubbled wall. A column of deep black smoke corkscrewed into the blue sky. The mine. After a few moments, the smoke thinned into a loose grey haze that blanketed the surrounding mountains. The haze hid the origin of the explosion as well as Gazan's fighters, who surely watched from some fold in the rock or gathering of pines.

We stood silently until the villagers climbed down from the roofs and went back to their work. Atal turned towards me. In the daylight I could see the tired shadows that hung beneath his eyes.

It's grown so late it's morning, he said. I'll see you when it's dark again.

We shook and placed our palms over our hearts, as is the custom with friends. I left for Mumtaz's home. On the way, I passed a number of villagers. None of them paid me notice. They'd accepted the outside world intruding on their lives. But as they walked by, I felt a certain kinship with their resignation. It was the same resignation I felt towards Commander Sabir. He'd done nothing to stop the attack I'd warned him about. And I'd surely known the men who'd just been killed, but still, all I felt was numbness, the numbness of circumstances that can't be changed, unless we're reckless. Atal was reckless.

*

I collapsed in a pile by the stove. It was morning. Through the day I slept. Mumtaz came and went. Beyond my closed eyes, I felt his movements. He fumbled nearby, near the firewood, near his bed, close. He cooked lunch and left. Then he cooked dinner and left. He was there. I felt safe with him near, but I didn't want to face him. He wouldn't ask what I'd done the night before or where I'd been. He was too polite for that. Written into the lines of his face, as if in ink, was his knowledge of this war, and it would be difficult to look at him as I left to gain knowledge of my own.

I awoke after nightfall. Laid out next to me was a flat steel plate and on it an oily mound of chalow Mumtaz had prepared. The rice was slippery and still warm in my fingers. I shovelled it into my mouth with guilt. The old man hadn't cooked for himself. He'd cooked for me. Would I repay the generosity of one who'd sworn off badal to live a lonely peace, by killing Gazan, who claimed to want the same? But this was not the way to think. Mumtaz's brother was dead. Mine was alive. It is easy to fall into loneliness when the world has already fallen from you.

I wiped my greasy fingers against the hem of my shalwar kameez and left half the rice for Mumtaz. He didn't owe me all of it and I didn't want to owe him anything else.

I stepped outside. A warm wind spun a coil of dust across the courtyard. Leaning against the chicken coop, Mumtaz sat in the dark, staring a ways off. Iskander's head rested in his lap. I stood in the door of the main house. As I looked at Mumtaz, he turned away. He surely knew that no act of kindness could convince me to stay. So he said nothing, neither did I, and I left.

*

Atal's HiLux idled in the courtyard, echoing off the night. I climbed through the hole in his compound's outer wall. Here I saw Fareeda. She lay in the back of the house, the outline of her body etched in light from a lamp she used for her opium. Her black hair was uncovered. It spilled softly across her pillows. Her gaze rested somewhere in the darkness. I wasn't sure if she noticed me there. She exhaled a thick cloud of smoke. As it tumbled through the lamplight, I saw where the tangled flesh from her arm spread up her neck, unwinding just beneath the ear.

Before I could approach, Atal crossed the courtyard towards me. In each hand he carried a Kalashnikov. He pushed one into my chest. I flinched, taking a full step back. My hands were still slick with grease from the chalow and the gunmetal became slippery in them. The rifle forced a decision, one I wasn't ready to make. I no longer knew who I should be shooting at.

We'll take the north road to Shkin, said Atal. You drive. I'll keep watch. You know how to drive blacked out, yes?

Yes, with night vision, I replied.

Atal pointed towards the three-quarter moon. There is your night vision, he said.

I followed him into the HiLux, and slowly we drove through Gomal's dusty lanes. Atal whispered directions to me, his voice filled with a flat sameness that suited the colourless night of our journey. In the dark, we struggled to avoid the many mud-brick walls of the other compounds. Soon came our final turn out of the village, and a wide expanse of mountain lay before us. I slowed the truck and searched the distance for where we'd pick up the north road.

Atal grabbed my shoulder and pointed. There, he said.

A clean, flat stretch of earth unravelled from the far peaks like an inconvenient thread hanging loosely from a hem. It was the north road and it connected Gomal to the unkind world beyond.

We eased across the broken ground. Dust stuck to our windshield, obscuring everything. Atal hung from his waist out the passenger window. He looked for obstacles, shouting his corrections: Right turn! RIGHT TURN! and I'd jerk the wheel and we'd miss running into a boulder, or: Stop! STOP! and we'd brake just shy of dropping into a wadi. Every few seconds, I'd shoot windshield wiper fluid to clear my view. As Atal hung out the window, the fluid squirted into his face and he cursed, but he didn't tell me to stop. He knew I needed to see and I began to feel a fondness for him as we struggled across the broken ground together, me blind and his beard and shirt spotted with the blue soap.

After nearly thirty minutes, we planted our wheels on the hard-packed gravel of the north road. Now our truck sped from a crawl to a jog. Switchbacks carried us over the ridgelines. At times the rises were so steep it seemed as if the world had fallen away from us and we drove into the sky on a road of nothing. Then we'd crest a ridge only to descend, straining in first gear towards a stubborn earth that seemed determined to burrow us into it. At points the switchbacks became so narrow that the mountain rock clawed at our doors and we pulled our side mirrors in lest they snap off. For hours we drove like this. All that passed beside us was the mountain's face or the valley's drop, and between us was only silence.

Late in the night we climbed yet another switchback and crested yet another ridge. As the hood of our truck went from pointing at the stars to shuttling towards the valley floor, Atal's body shot up straight as a stalk. He grabbed me. AZIZ! he shouted. I stood with both feet on the brake pedal. We skidded forwards. The front of our truck dropped hard. I fumbled for the emergency brake, found it, and tugged with both arms. We tilted and stopped. Atal carefully leaned out his window. I did the same.

In front of us, on the road, a piece of earth had been scooped out and threatened to swallow our truck. Our two tyres hung over the crater's edge. I shifted into reverse, revved our engine, our wheels spun, our cab shook. Nothing. I tried once more. Again, nothing. Our truck balanced as scales do. Atal tapped my arm, opened his door a crack, and managed to slide out. I turned off the ignition and did the same. My door opened to a straight drop, nearly a hundred yards down the mountainside. I clung to the side of the truck as it crowded me against the small ledge. That's when I saw it. At the bottom of the mountainside was another truck. It'd been blown down there by whatever had cratered the road – the mine. The truck had flipped over and its chassis stared upward, frozen and useless, a mechanical death mask.

The three-quarter moon cast uneven shadows as we walked to the front of our truck and into the crater's bottom. Atal held his palm over the earth.

Still warm, he said.

I too held my palm above the earth and felt the warmth. I picked up the soil, rubbing its burned crust through my fingers. It felt oiled and sticky, a mix of engine grease, gasoline, and blood, most likely blood. Pressed against the far side of the crater was a door that had been blasted from the truck. Two vertical stripes were painted down it – Comanches. Relief tinged through me, a shameful sensation to have, but none of the Tomahawks had been killed, none of my closest friends, over a single fighting season that's what they'd become. Atal stood in the crater. Looking up, he examined our truck's chassis.

Even if we could back out, how would we turn around? he asked.

And I don't think we could reverse the whole way down, I said.

Agreed, he replied. Gazan's men did their job well.

Atal played with the opal around his neck, weighing our options. But nothing in his manner showed any thought to giving up and going back.

The north road will be closed until this is fixed, I said.

The words hung sadly between us. The north road would never be fixed. Who would fix it? No one. This loss was complete. We climbed out from the crater and stood on its lip. We were stuck. The road continued towards Shkin, but we'd never get our truck past the crater.

I told the American I'd come tonight, said Atal. He made the resolution to himself, but spoke it aloud. He tugged his beard, placed his hands on his hips, and headed for our truck.

Where are you going? I asked.

From the cab, he handed me one of the rifles. We're walking, he said.

I spoke, my words tangling together: We'll never make it before sunrise and to walk these roads with a rifle is—

Is dangerous? answered Atal. It is more so without one.

Perhaps we could—

He interrupted me again: Could what? Not go. We're going. How did you make it to Gomal, Aziz?

I walked, but not the whole way.

Yes, he said, so we'll begin walking. Hopefully we'll have more luck than your friends in that truck. If we do, we won't have to walk the whole way.

Atal climbed into the crater and ran up its far side. He looked back at me. The scooped-out earth stood between us. I followed him across and we continued silently along the north road's shoulder as it descended into yet another switchback.

The night air was cool and clear. We passed over several more ridges. Neither of us spoke, silence being a precaution. We walked armed, afraid of those who prowled the mountains. Soon the terrain flattened and a dark pine forest crowded up to the road. Atal and I walked inside it, moving from trunk to trunk, concealed among the trees. Their branches cast shadows through the moonlight and we struggled to keep the road in sight from the forest's edge. Every ten minutes or so we'd stop, crouch next to a tree, and strain to hear a branch snap underfoot or a chest cough along the road. Our progress was careful, slow, and held no promise of bringing us to Shkin before sunrise.

An engine's noise broke the silence.

I froze.

Atal turned and bounded from trunk to trunk, until he crouched next to me. His gaze fixed on mine. He said nothing, but nodded, as though his nod made real what we both knew. There was someone ahead.

I'll approach, he said in less than a whisper, but more than a breath.

Special Lashkar, I mouthed the words, asking both a question and giving what I thought to be the answer.

Or Gazan's men, he said.

Leave your rifle, I hissed.

He shook his head, saying: I won't be shot without my rifle.

Before I could say anything else, he weaved quickly between the pines. The dead needles on the forest floor gave beneath his feet, muffling his heavy steps. I followed him at nearly a run. But as he crossed the boundary between the forest and the road, I stopped and knelt at the last tree. Slowly, from the ground, the damp from the pine needles crept up my leg. Steam rose from my body in the cool air. I wondered if anyone could see me. I looked down the road. They'd see Atal before they ever saw me.

Atal slung his rifle over his shoulder, showing he meant no harm. In the distance, the truck was pulled along the road's edge, where a switchback turned to climb a ridge. Atal continued his approach. His steps were slow and smooth. Heel to toe, heel to toe. Moonlight glanced off the truck's windshield. Soon Atal's silhouette merged with the glare. Heel to toe, heel to toe. The bed of the truck burst to life. Something swung towards him.

On the ground! a voice screamed. Put it on the ground!

In rhythm with his steps, Atal swung the rifle off his shoulder. He laid it in the dirt. Calmly, he called back: I have business on your firebase. I am Atal.

Firebase.

The truck was from the Special Lashkar. Heel to toe, heel to toe. Atal wouldn't stop. Go no farther! shouted the dark figure in the bed. STOP! The man's shouts had become a shriek. He fumbled with what I could now see was a machine gun. The cab's doors swooped opened like broad, vengeful wings. Another two figures stepped out. Atal was going to be shot.

I dropped my rifle and ran from the edge of the forest to the road. DON'T SHOOT! I shouted. WE'RE TOMAHAWKS! The machine gunner levelled his barrel on me. I grimaced, tucked my chin to my chest, but kept running. One of the men who'd stepped from the cab jerked the machine gun's muzzle towards the ground – *crack, crack* – the report of the gun.

I breathed. I looked up. I was fine.

Atal stood next to the truck bed. His elbows now hung over its side as if he'd paddled to the edge of a swimming pool. He gazed up at the machine gunner. I have business on your firebase, he repeated. I am Atal.

The man who'd stepped from the cab's open door ran to the back of the truck. He moved past Atal, vaulted over the tailgate and into the bed. He extended himself up on his toes, hung for a moment in the air, and slammed his fist into the machine gunner's jaw. There was another, duller, *crack* and the machine gunner collapsed. The man hissed after him: Who told you to shoot?

I knew the voice – Yar.

I charged towards the truck. In the darkness the forms around it took shape. Yar stood in the bed and rubbed the three knuckles of his clipped rooster hand. Atal looked up at him, about to announce himself yet again. Another man walked from the far side of the cab and around the truck's front – Mortaza.

It's me, Aziz! I shouted to my old comrades.

Yar called along the road: Aziz? What business do you have here?

Then Yar glanced down to where Atal smugly leaned against the HiLux's bed, my business clearly tethered to his. I have an important matter to discuss on your firebase, said Atal. We'd like to get to Shkin tonight.

Really? said Yar. Us too. But our orders are to man this checkpoint for the next two days.

The road behind us is impassable, said Atal. A mine's blown a crater into it. I imagine you know this. Our truck is stuck there.

It seems your work now hinders you, snorted Yar.

My work! said Atal. The mines target your checkpoints and would not be here if not for you.

As they argued, Mortaza planted himself silently beside me. He grabbed the meat of my arm and gave it a squeeze. I nodded and he smiled. The machine gunner in the bed stood. His smooth face, soft lashes, and wide round eyes undermined his tough veneer. He rolled his jaw and cringed as fresh pain shot through it.

Yar took a break from arguing with Atal and cursed the machine gunner: You fool. You nearly killed the man you replaced on this gun. This is Aziz.

The machine gunner gave me a restrained smile that didn't hurt his jaw, but offered no real friendship. He was a new arrival and I wondered where in his chest lived that hard little pit which had brought him to the Special Lashkar.

Why do you need to go back to the firebase? Mortaza asked me softly.

Atal and Yar stopped arguing. They looked at me.

I'm helping Atal get there, I said. I work for him now. It is safer to come and go at night, especially for me, since my accident.

My last word hung in the air, awkwardly.

Yar looked in the direction we'd come from, towards the crater. You're right, he said. This road is dangerous. But the firebase isn't as dangerous for you now. It was Qiam's truck that hit the mine.

We stood in the night air. Their HiLux's engine idled, its low rumble the only sound. All eyes rested on mine, searching for my reaction to this black blessing. The end of Tawas and Qiam's bloodline ended the badal against me, but took from some larger whole, one that I could only feel, and just like the crater that would never be repaired, this loss was complete.

I am sorry, I said, my words more prayer than apology.

Yar nodded. Our instructions are to hold this checkpoint, but I'll call back to see what can be done.

He climbed into the HiLux.

The machine gunner sat in the bed. He tilted his head back against the cab. The static hiss of the radio rose and fell over the idling engine. Atal walked up the road to where his rifle still lay in the dirt. Mortaza turned to me. All this time, you've been in Gomal, he said.

I nodded.

How is it? he asked.

Choked by checkpoints and Gazan's mortar attacks.

Perhaps we'll get off these checkpoints soon, said Mortaza. Then Commander Sabir can build his outpost and we can hunt down Gazan.

Perhaps.

We need to. Otherwise . . . otherwise, what will be done . . . ?
His voice trailed off.

What happened to Puskie? I asked.

I take care of him now, answered Mortaza. Yar still wants
Naseeb to cook him for dinner, he says he can't stand his cackling.
But he just likes to complain.

Tawas would be happy about that.

About Puskie being alive or about Yar being annoyed? he
asked.

Both, I think.

I still lie in bed and listen to him, said Mortaza. Always the
same, that's what I like most about his song.

Yes, always the same, I said. You just need a stick to keep
Puskie going.

Atal returned up the road, a rifle over each shoulder – he'd
found mine as well. There is very little time, he announced. It
is important that we arrive in Shkin tonight.

Yar stepped from the cab. I spoke with Commander Sabir,
he said. We are to take the two of you back with us.

Atal's expression fell. He seemed disappointed that
Commander Sabir was now involved. But still, the two of
us approached the open doors of their HiLux. Yar stopped
us with an outstretched hand. He lifted the rifles off Atal's
shoulders. You can both ride in back, he said. These will ride
inside with us.

Atal cast a sour look at Yar, who responded by throwing his
thumb towards the bed. We climbed over the tailgate and the
young machine gunner cleared a small space for us between the
crates of ammunition and water jugs. Atal and I sat in the bed,
unarmed, with our knees pressed to our chests. The cold crawled
into us. The HiLux shuddered into gear and I drew my legs up

close for warmth. We accelerated along the north road and when the first gust of cool air turned to a frozen rush no one spoke.

★

The night passed and the three-quarter moon slipped down the sky, disappearing behind the jagged mountains. The north road wove through endless ridges, each one proof that Atal and I were fools, for only fools would've tried to make this journey on foot. Dawn's first thin glow soon showed the pale silhouette of the firebase. Rows of HESCO bulged with earth. They formed the familiar perimeter that sat, as if a crown, on a mountaintop that without it would be like any other. Our truck shifted into a low gear to climb the last few switchbacks. We made a final turn and the red and white arm of the entrance's gate appeared in full view. It had already been raised, our arrival expected.

We crossed into the HESCO perimeter. Behind us, the guard closed the gate arm, pulling a strand of worn rope that hung from its end. It banged heavily, jarring the young machine gunner awake. We parked our truck and he stood in the bed, stretching his cold and stiff body. Atal and I did the same. As we stood I saw Commander Sabir across the firebase's courtyard, planted in front of his quarters. Light poured from his doorway and cast shadows on his face as he considered the nature of our visit.

Aziz! shouted Yar from the cab. Commander Sabir wants to speak with you.

As I climbed from the truck, I nervously kept my gaze to the ground, worried by all the duplicity I understood, and all that might be revealed if Commander Sabir or Atal looked too deeply into my wavering eyes. I crossed the courtyard and felt Atal willing me to silence from behind – I had full knowledge of his plot with Gazan. Commander Sabir walked back into his quarters and left the door open, an invitation for me to follow. On the far side of the firebase I glimpsed another light. It came from the small hut in the corner with a black HiLux parked out front. Inside, a figure paced behind a shut door, breaking up the light. It was Mr Jack. He waited for Atal.

★

Commander Sabir reclined against his bed. I shut the door and sat cross-legged on the floor in front of him. On the end table next to his pillow was the fishbowl. It was empty except for the many-coloured rocks that still filled its bottom.

Where's Omar? I asked.

Dead, answered Commander Sabir.

Dead?

He held me with his stare as if wrestling to pair words with events. Then he said: Mr Jack's been busy elsewhere, neglecting to visit, so I ran out of fish food. Omar didn't eat for many days. When he began to starve, I fed him rice. It made him very sick.

I imagined one-eyed Omar feasting on the rice, the grains expanding in his fish stomach, exploding it. Commander Sabir's eyes wandered the room, no longer meeting mine, and in their avoidance I saw his little shame at being unable to care for his companion. For him, I felt sorry, but for Mr Jack, I felt something meaner.

But he gave you Omar as a gift? I asked.

Mr Jack is quickly distracted, he said.

This is poor manners, I answered.

You talk of manners, he replied. You who journey here without my permission and who bring an unannounced guest.

There was no time to tell you, I muttered.

From beneath his bed, he pulled out a bottle that was empty but for a splash of Jim Beam. He frowned, dumping what was left into two paper cups. You had time to warn me about the mine on the north road, he said.

And you did nothing to stop it, I replied with anger in my voice.

And you have not thanked me for that, he spit back. The skin across his face pulled taut. His exposed teeth jutted from his mangled lower lip, his expression lost in the violence of his face. Doubt turned inside me. Commander Sabir offered me a cup. Do you believe it was an accident that was Qiam's truck? he asked. Think what you will of me, Aziz, but I am deliberate.

My words knotted in my mouth as I spoke them: The feud was between us, not you . . . he and I were friends before.

All I said dribbled from my lips in a trail of embarrassing innocence.

He would have killed you as a friend, but I am commander of all this, he said, waving his arms around the room. You are more valuable to me than he is. You have access to Atal and you, I think, already know his plans. And don't forget this last fact, Aziz, as long as you take money from me, for your brother, you are still a soldier.

I don't need to be reminded of that, I said, and swallowed from my cup.

Good, he replied. Then, as a soldier, give your report.

I drank again.

Atal isn't supporting Gazan's fight against you, I said.

Then what is the nature of their business? he asked.

Atal is brokering a peace between Gazan and the Americans.

As I told him this, I paused, searching for any sign of what he thought of such news. He offered none. I continued: Gazan is tired of fighting. When he met with Atal at the madrassa it was to discuss this peace. That's why we've come today. Atal is speaking with Mr Jack about a deal for Gazan.

I looked away from Commander Sabir and down into my Jim Beam. The alcohol had sunken into its seams, reacting with the glue, staining the paper wet, but there was no wetness to speak of, just the stain. I wondered if the whisky stained my insides the same. I took another sip and it burned down my throat.

You must have met Gazan and his fighters, he said. What do you make of them?

They're feral men, I answered. You've kept them hungry and you give them just enough to be controlled. Food, weapons, an enemy, I know you give all that to them.

And what of it, Aziz! he snapped, his head cocked to the side. War is a contest of wills. If I supply my opponent, I control his will, and the war with it.

A thing such as this never ends.

Are you fighting this war to end it? he spoke through a smirk.

I shook my head, ashamed that I no longer knew how to answer.

You fight for badal, to avenge Ali, and to support him in the hospital, said Commander Sabir. What happens if our war ends?

He drank from his cup and sat on the edge of his bed.

I'm just a soldier caught up in this, I replied.

All are caught up in this, he said. The question is whether you'll be a victim or prosper in it. What justice is there for you if Gazan, who crippled your brother, prospers in peace with the Americans? What justice is there if we lose control of him and never build our outpost? Yes, there will be peace for Gomal and Gazan, but us, what of us? The Americans will no longer need us. How do we survive then?

Commander Sabir reached under his bed, knocking his empty cup on the floor. He fumbled beneath for a moment and brought out a slim black pistol, a Makarov. He placed it in front of me.

We have a plan, he said. Our plan is to prosper. Take badal against Gazan, for your brother, and for me, who first offered you hospitality in this war.

I picked up the Makarov. Its heft sunk into my palm, and I felt the permanence of its metal. A pistol's purpose was the same as a rifle's, but achieved so casually. A rifle requires the whole body to fire it. Laying the buttstock into the shoulder, leaning against the recoil, concentrating on the sights, all of this draws from every part of the shooter. But with a pistol, just a flick of the wrist and a light twitch with an index finger delivers a hard bullet.

And what of Atal? I asked.

You know the answer to that.

His words chilled the air, reminding me of the night I'd first met Gazan and the fear I'd felt in the high forest just below the ridgetops covered with snow.

My badal is only against Gazan, I said.

And you'll have it, he answered. I've given it to you and you should be grateful, but remember there is a cost.

Badal is a just vengeance, I said. This cost isn't just.

Commander Sabir spoke, thrusting his finger in my face: Atal will lie down with any dog to keep his village from choosing a side. If you want Gazan the cost is Atal. Gazan for your badal, Atal so the Special Lashkar may prosper. That is just. Don't think for a moment Atal won't kill you for interfering with his plans. Remember, he is Hafez's cousin and part of that kinship which killed my brother and crippled yours.

And Haji Jan? I asked. He was not part of that kinship.

Very good, he said. Now you see the way of it. Commander Sabir almost grinned: No, Haji Jan was a stubborn old fool. A different choice by him at the shura, and he would be alive, and I would have my outpost, and Gomal would be prospering beneath my protection.

Killing him left you with Atal, I said. He is more against the outpost than any.

Yes, and if Gazan had done his errand properly that day, Atal would've joined Haji Jan. But now you will finish what Gazan started for me.

Commander Sabir's sweet, boozy breath hung on my face. A soapy film of drunkenness coated his eyes, but then, when I stood and tucked the Makarov under my shalwar kameez and into my waistband, his stare moved with sharp flashes, like water crossed by wind.

With respect, I must excuse myself, I said. Atal will grow suspicious if he finishes with Mr Jack and I'm still here with you.

Of course, answered Commander Sabir. You have work to do. I've arranged a truck to help tow your vehicle from the crater. It will meet you at the gate.

I thanked him and walked towards the door. The Makarov rubbed against my back, falling in rhythm with my steps.

Aziz, he called after me. By the time you complete your task, I should have some news of your brother.

I paused at the door and glanced back.

Commander Sabir had climbed down on his hands and knees. He peered at the empty bottles beneath his bed, searching for some forgotten splash of Jim Beam. I left him to his search and stepped into the night, towards the dimly lit hut that held Atal and Mr Jack.

I RUSHED ACROSS THE COURTYARD. Atal was still inside with Mr Jack. I stood by the door, but I couldn't make out the details of their conversation, for they spoke in quick whispers. Still, the tension in their words seeped through the cracks in the hut's plywood frame.

I leaned against Mr Jack's truck, settling in for a long negotiation. It was the same model HiLux as Atal's but larger. The bed was higher, the wheels taller and wider, and from where our mechanic had washed it, the black paint reflected what little light there was. I glanced into the back where empty shell casings, their primers dented and mouths dusted by soot, spread across the bed like a loosely knit shawl. I wondered if Mr Jack had been in a fight on his way here or if these were left over from some other engagement. American rifle rounds are sharp, thin, and elegant compared to our Soviet Bloc ammunition. I picked up an unfired round among the empty ones, twirling it in my fingers.

The door to the hut flew open, and Mr Jack stepped outside, blindly. His sun-bleached eyes looked into the night, and it took him a moment to find his HiLux. Once he did, he saw me leaning against its tailgate.

Hey, sport, finger-fuck somebody else's shit!

He shooed me away as though I were a beggar. Then he cranked on the ignition and sped out of the firebase's gate.

Atal stepped from the door behind Mr Jack.

Come, Aziz, time to find a way home.

Commander Sabir has arranged for some of his soldiers to help us recover our vehicle, I said. We're to meet them at the gate.

Very generous of him, replied Atal with a frown. Is that what he wanted to speak to you about?

That, and he told me even with Qiam dead, I still shouldn't come here. He thinks it would be better if I left Gomal and returned to Orgun.

I lied.

This firebase isn't a good place for either of us, said Atal.

He walked towards the front gate and I followed close behind. At the gate we sat, huddling into ourselves to ward off a chill made worse by exhaustion. Down by the motor pool, energetic voices called out over an engine that rolled warmly against the morning air. Soon a grey HiLux bounced down the gravel road and towards us. It stopped, followed by a trail of dust, which settled on Atal and me as if it were baking flour. The driver rolled down his window and threw a thumb towards the back. Any hope we'd had of a comfortable ride in the cab vanished. We climbed into the steel bed next to a heavily bundled machine gunner. His face was covered with a thick black balaclava, but beneath it, I knew there was only that unfeeling expression which is all hardship. Atal and I sat in the icy bed and drew our legs to our chests.

We bumped and jarred down the north road and our heads hung towards our bodies, limp with cold. Progress was measured not in the distance covered but by the sun as we climbed the surrounding ridges. Its rays greeted our chilled bodies as we arrived at each peak and our heads lifted from our chests, our skin inhaling the warmth that would stay with us along the first part of our descent. Then we'd weave down into the cool shadow. Here, our heads fell back to our chests, the green-needled pines darkened, and the night air in the valley lingered despite the day. But the day's progress worked to our advantage, and by late morning the sun sat atop a hard blue sky of its own invention.

Soon the warmth of the day overtook me. I drifted. I drifted towards my brother. I thought of him in his hospital bed. The nothingness of his amputated flesh dissolving his spirit, until all that remained were ashes heaped on the imprint of his body. Before, when Ali and I had no home and it rained, we'd huddle in doorways. If I ever complained, he'd grab my arm and ask: Are you made of sugar? Will you melt? His words would be firm, but he'd always end with a smile that added some warmth to the damp. Now I thought of him, melting. I imagined walking into his hospital room, whispering in his ear about how I'd killed Gazan, and in that moment, when he knew what I'd done, I'd watch his spirit set and return to him as though a thickener were added to that same ash heap.

I raised my head and gazed at Atal, his hands crossed over his knees, his head hanging between them. Tucked into himself, he looked like a bridge that had collapsed under some unseen weight. This tangle of a man endured the living insult to his nang that was Commander Sabir. And it was that insult, and the endurance to bear it, that made me uncertain whether I admired or pitied him. Atal could've taken Hafez's place. He could've led the fighters in those mountains instead of Gazan. Atal defied all that and he defied Pashtunwali. There was arrogance to such defiance. Life would have been better for his village if he'd taken badal, and with it taken Hafez's place, and truly fought against

Commander Sabir, not as a lackey like Gazan, who took food, weapons, and ammunition, but in a true fight. No deceit.

The arrogance. I held onto the thought. I'd kill Gazan for badal, but I could kill Atal for his well-meaning arrogance.

We climbed yet another steep switchback and our truck jolted to a stop. I toppled against my side, so did Atal. The machine gunner fell from his perch on two ammunition cans, his ass making a vertical drop of nearly a foot. There was a dull thud then a groan. I imagined the machine gunner's face beneath his balaclava, in pain but still without expression.

Atal now stood in the bed. He banged on the roof of the cab and pointed ahead of us. There it is! he called out.

Our stranded truck sat atop the ridgeline, its front still balanced unsteadily over the crater's edge. We pulled up to the crater and our work began. We used shovels, picks, and even a helmet to dig at its lip. The ground beneath us was brittle. The mine had blown to shards any large rocks that might have hindered us. Soon we'd dug out enough of the lip to flatten it so the front axle's tyres rested against the earth.

Our truck was now set to back out. This would be the most dangerous part, reversing down the steep and narrow switchback. All of the Special Lashkar's trucks had a winch in front – two hundred or so feet of steel cable wrapped tightly around a motor that could pull a tree from its roots. The soldier wearing the balaclava hooked his winch under the front axle of Atal's HiLux. On the far side of the crater, the driver took in all the slack. In theory the winch would lower us along the tight switchbacks and ensure that we didn't topple down the mountainside, but the driver took no chances. He left his door open and both his legs dangled from the side of his seat. If he had to jump he'd be ready, even as his truck, as well as ours, toppled into the ravine below. Whoever drove our truck would have to sit behind the steering wheel. This made jumping a more difficult prospect.

With the winch set, the soldier wearing the balaclava raised his arm and gave a thumbs-up. He then looked at Atal and me. We had yet to decide who would drive. I started out towards the truck, but Atal grabbed my arm and stopped me. He sat behind the steering wheel instead. What a strange thing that he placed enough value on my life to offer a chance against his own. I worked for him, and it would've been natural that he'd expect me to assume this risk, but serving Atal meant he also served you. This was how it was between us, and also how it was between him and the people of Gomal.

Atal shifted into reverse and the winch ground as the steel cables pulled taut. I shouted out directions: Come right, come right. Straight! STRAIGHT! Atal leaned his head out the driver's window. Then he shot across the cab, planting his face in the passenger's side mirror. He continued to weave back and forth in this way as we inched out our descent. The winch strained and the steel cable slid against our front axle. The air filled with a hot metal burn. We soon dipped out of sight from the soldiers above us, but we were still tethered to their winch. I continued to shout my directions and Atal, unable to see the space around our truck, followed each one blindly: Come left. Straight. Now, right, right! RIGHT!

We reached the intersection of the two switchbacks. Here the road thickened. Atal backed up and turned the truck down the mountain, facing forwards and out of danger. I dropped beneath the fender and untied the steel cable from our front axle. All clear! I called above us. The winch's motor quickly engaged and with a high whine the steel cable slithered up the hill, snaking on the dirt. Atal stepped from the cab and offered me his seat as though it were a valued prize. I shuffled along the narrow ledge between the driver's-side door and the ridgeline's sheer face. I stared at my feet. A hundred yards beneath my toes were the remains of the truck that had struck the mine. Rust already spread over the chassis, beginning the earth's slow gestation of the metal. Somewhere down there was Qiam. The earth would consume his flesh more quickly than it would the wreckage, but eventually everything would be consumed.

Returning along the north road, our truck kicked up a dust cloud announcing us to anyone who lurked in the miles of surrounding ridgelines. Driving during the day was dangerous but quick. We crested a final rise. From here, we could see the mud walls of Gomal drawn into the dirt valley below. It all appeared close, but was still miles away.

A difficult but worthwhile trip, yes? said Atal.

Yes, I said, difficult.

Worthwhile for you?

I kept my eyes on the road as I spoke: If it was for you, then yes.

I needed to see the American, he replied.

And the American, he seemed upset when he left?

Atal offered no answer. Had I overstepped? He stroked his beard, while I concentrated on driving. As the last switchback spilled into the valley, we entered the road's final dusty stretch. Atal gazed out the window. He rattled a bottle of pills in his pocket and spoke again: He couldn't have been too upset. He gave me Fareeda's medicine. I would say he was disappointed. They have a different sense of time than us, rushing all things. This often leads to disappointment.

What was he disappointed about? I asked.

226

He wants to be involved in things he has no business being involved in, explained Atal. He wants to meet Gazan. He wants his plans to move quicker than they should. But I made progress today with the American. I think life will be getting better in our village.

So, he has never met Gazan? I asked.

No, he said, and as long as I can I'll keep it this way. The Americans believe that if they give you something they can take everything. That makes them dangerous friends.

He looked at me through the sides of his eyes. There was nothing more to say. Soon we arrived in Gomal, where late-afternoon shadows cast down from the walls of the compounds, greeting us darkly. We pulled next to Atal's home and I turned off the engine. The two of us sat in the silence of the cab, unmoving and exhausted. After a few moments, Atal spoke: Don't worry about cleaning up the truck, Aziz. I'll take care of it in the morning.

I was grateful for this, but to reinforce my status as his employee, he reached into the pocket of his shalwar kameez and from it pulled an envelope filled with crisp US dollars. He peeled off a few bills and pressed them into my hand.

For your work before and for today's work, fair? he asked.

Yes, thank you, I said.

Good, he replied. There is more to be done, but now we rest.

He stepped from the truck and towards his front door. For a moment longer, I sat alone in the cab. Then I stuck the crisp bills in my pocket, next to my cell phone. Before I left the truck, I reached to the small of my back and readjusted the Makarov that pressed there. I'd need to find a place to hide it.

As I went back to Mumtaz's home, the village streets filled with morning traffic. Dirt-faced children chased each other through the narrow lanes, their sweat forming mud canals down their reddened cheeks. Men, their stares downturned, heaved wheelbarrows full of grey-branched wood, blond straw bundles, and slabs of scrap metal to sell at the bazaar. The dingy shopfronts seemed like the chambers of some great communal heart, which today pumped the commerce of optimism through all Gomal. I felt like an imposter as I walked among the villagers. I hadn't slept and therefore hadn't awoken to whatever hopefulness these people had found. I was a remnant of yesterday and last night.

Mumtaz's gate was unlocked. It clanged as I swung it open. I was grateful to get off the street. As I crossed the courtyard, Iskander stuck his head out from the chicken coop. His ears were pinned back anxiously but relaxed on seeing me. He returned to his shaded coop and continued his nap. Exhaustion felt like a dull itch in my eyes. I entered the house and wanted to collapse on its dirt floor. Empty stillness rang in my ears. I was grateful for the solitude. The old man would've filled the space between us with his suspicions, even if he never said a word. But whatever sharp thing I felt towards him softened when I saw he'd left a dish of food out for me.

I stretched along my foam sleeping mat and hungrily scooped fistfuls of rice into my mouth. Cold grease covered each grain. The dirt on my face soon mixed with it to form a slick and gritty film that spread across my lips and cheeks. I smeared the mess on my sleeve and settled into my bed. The previous night's chill still clung to me and my fleece-lined blanket slowly absorbed it. I was filthy but content as I lay in Mumtaz's house and in his care.

I rolled onto my side and the Makarov stuck at my back. With one last bit of energy, I rose to my feet and looked for a place to hide it. Neither the blankets nor the mats strewn across the floor, nor the stove, nor the pots and pans we cooked from offered any good option. The room was bare and without possibilities. In the corner next to me was the pile of firewood. This would have to do. I pulled apart the branches and restacked them with the Makarov hidden beneath. As I crept back to the warmth of my bed, I wondered how soon it would be before I'd need to use it. I doubted it would be long.

★

Then the war left the village.

Whatever Atal had negotiated between Gazan and Mr Jack seemed to bring the peace. Days and then weeks passed with no mortar attacks, no mines on the north road, nothing. During this time Atal never called on me. Every few days, I'd leave in the morning to gather firewood in the high forest. Once in the mountains, I'd steal off behind the large boulder and pull the phone from my pocket. There was never a message from Commander Sabir and I felt no desire to leave him one. I'd return at night and as I added to the stack of firewood, I added to my confidence that the Makarov would never be found. But I also added to my doubts, doubts that I'd have the chance to use the Makarov and doubts that I even wanted to.

Around the warm stove, Mumtaz still spun large stories of his youth. He'd smile easily and mutter happily about the old days, his brother, and trips with his father to places I'd never heard of or only imagined. He told these stories with a certain hope, as if the memories he welcomed could destroy the memories he didn't. As these new days rolled out in front of us, the villagers accepted them with a similar hope, as though days of peace could destroy memories of war.

After dinner one night Mumtaz reclined on his bed. He chewed on a bone from a scrap of lamb we'd mixed with the rice to make a qorma. Aziz, he said, where did you get that ring of yours?

I've always had it, I told him.

So it came from your family, said Mumtaz. That is good. I have nothing of my family, except for this. He framed his face with his hands and said: My good looks!

I'm not as good-looking as you, I answered. So my family gave me the ring.

He laughed and I relaxed a bit.

The stone is a ruby, is it not? he said. Was it your father's?

And my brother's after that.

Your brother is dead?

Why do you say that?

If you wear your father's ring, he said. I would think it meant your brother is dead.

He's not dead.

For a moment after I answered, it became quiet between us. If he no longer wears the ring, said Mumtaz, then you've taken his place in your family.

I could never take his place, I said, and emotion filled my words, surprising me. To take Ali's place was to accept all we'd lost.

No, of course, said Mumtaz. He looked away from me and gazed towards the wall of firewood. Again he spoke: The peace these last few weeks, it feels like living in a new memory.

Yes, I said, new memories to replace the old ones.

I don't think they'll replace the old ones, he replied.

You shouldn't speak so.

Mumtaz grabbed my shoulder and pointed to where the firewood concealed the Makarov. He answered: Whatever thing you've hidden there makes it so.

I gave the old man a sharp look. I had only lies and I wouldn't respond with these. I am old, not blind, said Mumtaz. This peace brought by Atal and the American is a bad one. What you've chosen to hide will destroy it.

I said nothing else. Neither did he. We slept in his room built of mud.

The next morning, Mumtaz left to wander the bazaar. He asked if I wished to join him. I never did, but always he asked. As soon as he left, I unstacked the firewood and tucked the Makarov into the small of my back. I'd carry it there until Atal called.

I walked into the courtyard. The hard mechanics of the pistol stuck into me with every movement. Iskander stepped from the chicken coop with his ears pinned back and his head cocked. He gave me a moment's consideration. A dog always knows what's hidden, and his ears now pointed straight up. He turned away from me. He then trotted back to the moulted air of the chicken coop, preferring it to my company.

Carrying the Makarov this way couldn't be sustained. I wanted an end and badal. And the pistol, with its ever present sticking, made me all the more certain that Atal's next call would come. Soon it did.

*

With the Makarov tucked into my waistband, I slept only in fits and starts. I dreamed of it going off, crippling me as my brother had been, or of awakening with it lying out for Mumtaz to see.

In my dreams I saw the old man's face, disappointed but never surprised. I slept like this for only a few nights. In the middle of one, a glare washed everything out and then there was a kicking at my feet. I awoke. Out by the coop, Iskander howled but was too afraid to confront whoever held the light that shined down on me.

Come, Aziz. There is work to be done.

The voice was Atal's.

I put my hand up to block the light.

Who do you think you are, barging into my home like this! grumbled Mumtaz.

Your friend and I have business, said Atal. Then he turned to me: Hurry.

I rose and fixed my shalwar kameez. The Makarov still poked in my waistband, a reminder of my commitments.

Mumtaz grasped my leg. He said: You don't have to, Aziz . . .

Have you enjoyed the peace as of late, old man? snapped Atal.

Mumtaz stared back stupidly. I couldn't tell if he was considering the question or startled by the flashlight that flushed out his vision. He held an upturned palm towards his eyes. Of what importance is this? he asked.

You are right, none, said Atal. What is important is that Aziz must come.

I nodded.

Aziz! Mumtaz called after me.

He stood from his bedding, his stocking feet planted sadly on the fleece blanket. I turned towards him. He struggled with his words: I hope you'll return here – instead of where else you might go.

I clasped each of his shoulders and held him in front of me. Of course, baba, I said. Then the two of us embraced. The meat of his forearms brushed against the Makarov. I knew he felt it, but he didn't flinch. What passed between us had no deception in it. And as I left, I wanted to return to him.

Outside the courtyard wall, the white HiLux idled warmly. We climbed inside and Atal leaned over the steering wheel. His eyes were wide. He seemed determined not to blink until he'd made a full explanation. Tonight, he said, we have a meeting with Gazan. He paused for just a moment to see my response

I offered him none.

He'll be walking down the north road, explained Atal. You're to pick him up.

I nodded.

Once you do that, he said, drive back towards the village. I'll be on the side of the road waiting for you both and we'll have our meeting in the truck.

I nodded again.

Atal's eyes bulged wider.

The American is here, he said. He wants to meet you.

He blinked, shifted the truck into gear, and drove towards his house.

*

We pulled into Atal's courtyard, and the black HiLux I'd seen many times in Shkin was parked next to the dead generator. We walked inside. Mr Jack sat on the edge of the wide sofa, his elbows perched on his knees and his American rifle, an M-4, leaning against his leg. His shalwar kameez still held the creases from where it'd been folded in plastic packaging. A green T-shirt peeked from beneath its high collar and I could see where the cuff of his blue jeans snuck from beneath the traditional baggy trousers, the same worn by Atal and me. He stood as we entered and crowned his head with a wide Waziri-style pakol. The pakol framed his blond hair and faded blue eyes, making his whole face seem as happy and bright as a sunflower. His costume now complete, he extended his hand in friendship and spoke in Pashto: Aziz, I am Jack. Atal has told me all about you. I am glad for your help tonight.

I paused, gripped by the incredible whiteness of his teeth. I'd seen Mr Jack many times from afar in Shkin. He was a sort of celebrity to me. I gladly shook his hand, but as I did my awe of him melted away. His friendliness, American Pashto, and awkward wardrobe made him ridiculous.

I've explained our plan to Aziz, said Atal. He will do well.

Good, replied Mr Jack. You'll also help with security during the meeting.

That is fine, I said, shrugging my shoulders.

Mr Jack rested his eyes on mine for another moment, taking some last measure of me. Satisfied, he offered his white teeth again.

You are doing a great service for your village tonight, he told me, and I found it amusing that Mr Jack assumed Gomal was my village. He continued: We have to straighten things out around here. As a gesture of how grateful we are, I wanted to give you this ahead of time, for tonight's work.

Mr Jack handed me a yellow envelope. Inside it was a stack of hundred-dollar bills as thick as a small book. My eyes went wide and I struggled to restrain a surge of many emotions. This was nearly a year's salary in the Special Lashkar. With it I could lay the foundation of a new life, perhaps in Orgun, even as far away as Kabul. Money like this had the power to change everything.

Thank you, I muttered weakly.

No, thank you, said Mr Jack. Your efforts to bring peace to your home are worth more than this. I hope we can continue our relationship. It is important for us to have friends we can trust.

And, as friendly as he was, his tone made me feel very small.

Atal seemed interested but unimpressed by Mr Jack's advances. He watched our flirtation with the cynicism of a first wife who watches the courtship of the second. I tucked the envelope into my pocket, next to the few dollars Atal had paid me for the ride to Shkin some weeks before.

It is time, don't you think? Mr Jack asked Atal.

He nodded and handed me the keys to his HiLux.

Good luck, said Mr Jack. We'll see you shortly.

★

Unlike the last trip, I drove the north road with my high beams on. These two fans of light made the blackness everywhere else complete. I navigated the switchbacks, made aware of a climb or a descent only by whether or not I was pressed into my seat or pressed forwards into the steering wheel. Through the darkness, I travelled ten feet at a time and alone.

As I held the road's course, my mind shifted to Mr Jack and his money. In my pocket I held the promise of a future. In my back I had the Makarov and the promise of badal. The cost of killing Gazan would be Atal's life, and I couldn't kill Atal without also killing Mr Jack. I thought of Mumtaz and the silent peace we'd enjoyed since I'd returned. What if I abandoned Commander Sabir and worked for Mr Jack? I could eventually go back to Ali a wealthy man. Would wealth and the possibility of a new life be badal enough for my castrated brother, and for

235

me? Why should I kill Gazan when all it would give me was a future as Commander Sabir's slave? A year's pay. A pistol.

I opened the door and flung the Makarov into the night. End over end, it tumbled down the mountainside. If the chance for badal came again, maybe I'd take it. If the chance to earn money for a new life came, maybe I'd take that. But nothing was clear to me now, and I didn't want to act under the old certainties.

My HiLux suddenly jarred nose first into some hollow ground. The mine's crater. I looked off to my left, to the drop down the mountainside, and to where Qiam's body sat pinned beneath his truck, but I saw nothing except for the darkness that consumed everything. I shifted into a low gear, heaving myself up the crater's far side. Its sharp edges had become weather-beaten and smooth. Soon my HiLux gained enough tread to crest its lip. As it did, my headlights fell back against the road and washed over a dark figure – Gazan.

His slight body stood still and perfectly straight as though he were one of the pines that flanked the mountainside. He wore a black shalwar kameez, a black turban, and when you added to this his thick black beard, which started just beneath his eyes, he seemed swallowed by the night. He stared directly into my high beams and approached the passenger door with a confidence that unsettled me. He carried no rifle. He sat next to me in the cab and shut the door behind him. He began to knife his hand between the seat cushions, searching for something.

Where is my seat belt? he asked.

I don't think we have one, I replied.

Only a fool would travel these mountains without a seat belt. He opened the door as if refusing to come. Then, taking another look at me, he asked: I've met you before, haven't I? The one time in the forest, yes?

Yes, I said, one time in the forest.

Drive carefully, he demanded.

I nodded back. He shut his door and we set out towards Gomal.

One time in the forest, I thought. To figure so insignificantly was a small humiliation. If I ever took badal against him, it would be meaningless unless in that final moment he shared a complete understanding of how he'd impacted me. But maybe I didn't need to kill him, maybe if he just knew, that would be enough and then I could take Mr Jack's money and start again.

As I drove, I spoke: The first time we met was in the forest, but you knew of my brother before then.

Is that right? asked Gazan. Who is your brother?

Ali Iqtbal, I said, spitting out the name in a clenched hot voice that surprised even me. He is the reason I'm here with you.

What happened? asked Gazan. Did the Americans or Special Lashkar kill him? His tone was flat and uninterested. His eyes were focused more intently on the ground in front of us than on the conversation between us.

No, he's not dead. The war crippled him, or more specifically you did.

As I told him this, I felt as though I'd arrived at some destination, and I also fixed my stare at the headlights in front of us.

You must have a great anger towards me, said Gazan.

I said nothing.

And you want me to bring the peace? he asked.

I thought for a moment before I replied: Can you?

Gazan didn't answer this question but offered another: How was your brother crippled?

At the Ashura festival bombing, I said, nearly a year ago.

He rolled his eyes back, remembering, and nodded.

That was a difficult time, he said, and his words held no apology, as though my loss had been caused by some event of God outside his control, and perhaps it had been. Have you met Atal's American? he asked.

I nodded.

And are you for him? he replied.

It depends. If he can bring the peace, I'm for him.

Yes, the peace. We're all tired. And if I did the same?

And the words I spoke next surprised me: Then I could be for you.

What makes you think this American wants peace?

He spends money for it, I said. One can start again if there is enough money.

Gazan clutched at his beard, stroking it up to the knuckles, kneading at whatever wisdom lay inside. Perhaps, he said, but what you speak of is charity. Money is given for work. I don't know how to do the work Atal and the American ask.

But I thought you were for the peace? I replied.

Peace isn't built by soldiers, he said. It is built by others after the soldiers are gone. Men such as Sabir and me don't know how to bring peace and don't want to.

So you'll leave?

If I can, he answered. The only way this ends is if I leave and if all those who wish to fight leave. Peace will not come through us.

We continued to climb and descend the switchbacks, seeing no farther than the short reach of our headlights.

★

In the valley the driving became flat and predictable. Had it been day, Gomal would have sat low and dusty on the plain. I strained to see into the distance as we went, so too did Gazan. Both of us awaited the moment when Atal and Mr Jack would appear.

Soon we turned an easy bend in the road and Mr Jack's black HiLux came into view. Inside it, Atal's head rested against his arms, which hugged the steering wheel. He looked asleep. Mr Jack stood in the HiLux's bed with his American rifle slung against his chest and night-vision goggles pressed to his eyes. He scanned the north road with his back to us, searching in the wrong direction. Once we were on him, he turned with a start and waved in the air. He was excited and seemed almost surprised that his plan had come together so well.

We drove up next to them and stopped. Mr Jack flung open Gazan's door and took his hand, shaking it vigorously, in the American fashion.

Commander, welcome, he said.

Gazan reeled away, even as Mr Jack grasped his hand. All he could say was: You speak Pashto.

I speak good Pashto, replied Mr Jack.

Atal opened my door.

Sit in the back, he told me, behind Gazan. He handed me a Kalashnikov and said: For security.

The four of us climbed inside Atal's HiLux, leaving Mr Jack's truck on the shoulder of the gravel road. Gently, I pressed the muzzle of my rifle against the back of Gazan's seat, resting my finger on the trigger. My role in the meeting needed little explanation.

Mr Jack squeezed into the back next to me, our shoulders touching. Awkwardly, he propped his rifle between his legs, muzzle down, to show Gazan that he posed no threat. Atal shifted into gear and set out on the road. Mr Jack eagerly leaned forwards over the parking brake, beginning his negotiation with Gazan: When Atal told me about this meeting, I said I needed to come.

Atal, he is honourable man, said Gazan. He strained over his shoulder towards the back seat. Nods of appreciation passed between the three of them. Gazan continued slowly, speaking Pashto to Mr Jack like he was a child: Atal wants peace for his village. Atal resists Sabir and me the same and wants to end war. This is why I first approach him. He wants to end war. I want to leave war. Americans are most powerful. You can give me way to leave. That is why I talk to you.

Gazan emphasised the word *leave*, and Mr Jack nodded back, assuring him that he understood. Even though Gazan spoke to him like a child, Mr Jack didn't seem to notice. He opened his mouth to reply, but before he could, Atal interrupted with words of his own: Gazan has wanted to leave this war for some time. He is tired, but Sabir keeps him fighting for his own purposes. Sabir wants to build an outpost in our village. He says it's for our protection, but the construction contracts will fill his pockets. To justify the outpost, Sabir secretly supplies Gazan and keeps him on the attack, mortaring our village and mining our roads. Gazan, all respect to him, can do nothing against this. He must feed his fighters and make a living. Sabir can control him because he has money from you and the other Americans, but if Gazan makes peace with you, he can start a new life and my village can be left alone.

Gazan looked to Mr Jack, searching for his reaction to Atal's words.

I admire a man who wants peace for his village, said Mr Jack, and he grabbed the side of Atal's seat and patted him on the shoulder. He continued: And when I learned that you approached Atal, this did not surprise me. All respect him. But peace can only occur when all wish for it. Otherwise it is a false peace. Now is not that time. The war is bigger than one village and one group of militants. It still must be fought.

A confused silence fell through the truck. Atal continued to drive and as he did he spoke bitterly into the night: Some wars only feed themselves. They cannot be won, only starved.

Every war can be won, replied Mr Jack, but not every war is fought well. Commander Gazan, I have much respect for you and understand that you want to be finished with war. But your position is of great value to us.

I am done with fighting, said Gazan.

You will not have to fight, answered Mr Jack. You will only have to provide information to me about other Taliban and Haqqani militants. You will be well cared for

By whom? asked Gazan.

By us, said Mr Jack. You and your men will have better food, better weapons, and better pay. The supplies should still go through Sabir, but it is all by us. Of course, you will be compensated separately for the information you provide, and when you decide to leave, you'll have money to do so.

Atal accelerated his HiLux faster and faster down the road. We turned a corner and I had to grab Gazan's headrest to stay upright. My other hand still grasped the rifle. Its muzzle pressed into the back of Gazan's seat.

This offers no peace for Gomal! Atal pleaded. If Sabir builds his outpost, all there will be is war.

Yes, for a time, said Mr Jack. But with Gazan's information and militants flocking to attack a target like the outpost, we'll control much of the fighting.

Atal's eyes were wide and desperate. He drove even faster now, but barely watched the road. He spoke to Gazan: You came to me seeking peace. You can't be for this.

This is a way out for me, said Gazan. I am for this.

His response dropped from his mouth like a cold weight.

The restraint I'd felt towards Gazan left me. If the war was for him, he was for the war. If peace was for him, he was for peace. There could be nothing larger in him, and I felt the fool for hoping there could be, in him, in any of us. What moments before had seemed unclear was now obvious. There was no cause in this war, at least none larger than oneself. And what I did next was natural, and yes, easy.

The shot tore hotly through the back of Gazan's seat and covered the windshield in a red blossom. White stuffing feathered on the sticky glass.

Atal slammed on the brakes, blinded by the smear. The truck skidded to a stop.

Mr Jack fumbled with his rifle, its barrel stuck between his legs. He was clumsy as he struggled to lift it. The more he struggled, the more clumsy he appeared. I snapped the muzzle of my rifle up to his face and in that moment before I shot again, I looked into his eyes. The blue had all but left them. They were dry, the pupils hollowed and black, taking the last of the world in. The bullet went all the way through, shattering the window behind his head.

Atal clutched with panic at nothing. He had nothing. I paused for a breath. His death wasn't for me. It pained me, not because I cared for him, but because of Fareeda, Mumtaz, and the village. Who would care for their interests now? But this was the price Commander Sabir required for Gazan. I didn't know how he'd react to Mr Jack. That had not been discussed.

Across Atal's face, confusion formed in lines. My journey up to this moment – my brother, joining the Special Lashkar, Tawas's death – this was all invisible to him, but that invisible distance made my final action possible.

And when he slumped forwards and found his place against Gazan, it looked as if they'd finally embraced.

DEATH BRINGS WITH IT great stillness to those who are close by. I sat in the truck with the three of them for some time. Moments before, I hadn't even been certain I'd take badal against Gazan. Now that it was finished, I hoped the stillness would reveal what I should do next.

I sat very quietly.

I pulled the cell phone from my pocket and sent Commander Sabir a message: IT IS DONE, RETURNING. The *IT* I referred to was Atal. Commander Sabir didn't care about the other two. I'd killed Gazan for my badal. As for Mr Jack, another American would surely replace him, causing little interruption in Commander Sabir's plans. No one would know this killing had been a green on blue.

But as I thought about it, I felt uncertain it was. I no longer wore a uniform. Still, I'd been a member of the Special Lashkar, something the Americans made. I then recalled how Commander Sabir kept Gazan in business, and how the Americans kept Commander Sabir in business. And as I thought of all the ways one could be killed in this war, and of all those who could do it, I couldn't think of a single way to die which wasn't a green on blue. The Americans had a hand in creating all of it.

I opened the passenger side door and the overhead light came on, pasting its glare across the sweat, mucus, tears, and blood of a violent death. I pulled Gazan upright in his seat. Small wet flecks shined on his ashen face. His palms had fallen flat and upturned at his side. Only one thing surprised me, his eyes were closed. In that moment before his death, he seemed to decide that it was over, not me, and he shut his eyes. This robbed me of the idea that I took his life

I reached across Gazan's body and pulled Atal on top of him so I could drive. As I tugged at Atal, I noticed his silver chain with the opal had been split in two. I'd always admired the stone. Like so much of Atal, he'd bared this necklace to the world with a certain defiance, as if a precious stone, or even expensive clothes and a beautiful house, were talismans enough to protect his life from the dirt and need around it. I took the stone, tucking it in the pocket of my shalwar kameez. I could use a talisman.

My phone vibrated. A reply from Commander Sabir: RETURN.

Mr Jack's night-vision goggles had fallen between his legs. I picked them up and drove towards his black HiLux under their green glow. I parked Atal's truck next to Mr Jack's and pulled Atal's body back into the driver's seat. With the driver's door open, the overhead light gave me a last look at the scene and offered me confidence that whoever found this would draw a simple conclusion – a meeting between a militant commander, corrupt village elder, and overconfident American gone sour with deceit. The near truth of it would've left me satisfied, but for one thing, Fareeda.

She'd soon learn of her uncle and imagine my role. I needed her to see the truth, as I knew it. There was time, I thought. If I hurried, I could make it to her and then travel to Shkin before daylight. I left the bodies and climbed into Mr Jack's HiLux. I began to drive. As I did, I stared across the valley, into the darkness where Fareeda's home was.

★

A light was on in the house. It flickered through the broken parts of the wall. It was a small light, but in the night there was none besides it. I parked the black HiLux by the red gate. I left the engine running. Outside, I slung the Kalashnikov on my shoulder. Its muzzle faced the ground. As I walked, my leg brushed against its warm barrel. I stepped through the wall and went towards the house.

The door was open. In the breeze its hinges creaked. Just past it was the bare flame of an oil lamp. I stood in the dark-ness of the doorway and saw Fareeda. She sat on the sofa in the living room, waiting, it seemed. I thought of the story Atal had told me, about how he'd found her in this same room when she was a girl. This was the second time she'd been abandoned here. But I knew it was worse than this. If she waited for him tonight, it meant she waited for him always. And each time he left she was abandoned.

I stepped inside, to where she could see me. Her eyes found mine but quickly left them, instead finding the rifle on my shoulder. Only when I rested it by the door did her eyes return to mine. But still she said nothing. Instead she stood, took the lamp, and walked to the back of the house. I sat. In the dark-ness, I waited for her. Soon she returned. In her left hand, high above her head, she carried a tray. On it was a pot of tea with a single glass and the oil lamp. She placed the tray on the table and served me, pouring out the one glass. The lamp sat between us. I drank and, as we were close together in the light, she found the few dark stains of gore on my hands and clothes. This was what I'd come to tell her. There seemed no sense in hiding it, but before I could speak, she did.

You will stay now?

I shook my head, no.

Then you've killed me along with him, she said, looking towards the door. There, in the distant light of the lamp, dark and warm shadows cast strangely on the rifle. Use your rifle, she said. Come, do to me what it is you've already done.

I wish for something else, I answered. I looked away from her and into the lamp. I could be to you as he was, I said, if you let me find a way.

That way has taken my uncle from me, and before that my father, she replied.

I'll find the medicine you need.

After I spoke these words, her eyes rested on me hatefully. But it wasn't for Atal or for all that had been taken from her village. The hate was in the need. She was a prisoner of her needs, and I'd become the master of them. I loved her and so I'd find a way to care for her, but to care for her was to make her hate me. And looking at Fareeda, and all the beautiful and brutal parts of her body, I realised she'd hated Atal as well.

You'll return then? she asked.

I reached towards her. By instinct she moved away but stopped herself, letting me take. A shawl hung from her shoulders. The pads of my fingers skirted its hem, finding their way beneath. I touched the skin of her good arm. I wove my fingers through hers. Then, with my other hand, I pulled back the shawl. I clasped our palms together. I lifted her smooth hand up and kissed it as I'd seen Atal do before. I raised my head, searching for Fareeda's eyes, but she looked away. Her gaze rested coldly on the lamp between us. I reached over to the table and turned down its flame. In the darkness, she again shifted away from me. She was frightened of what I could and might do. I dropped her good hand from mine. With one arm, I pulled her towards me. Our bodies pressed against each other. Then hers became limp, as if she'd departed it, sacrificing herself to all the meanness she imagined in me. With my other hand, I reached across her and grasped the knotted flesh of her deformed arm. I held it up, as if I might kiss it too. But I couldn't.

Gently, I laid the arm across her lap. I pulled the hem of her shawl over it. From the pocket of my shalwar kameez, I took out the opal. I reached my arms around her neck. Behind her, I tied off the chain's two broken ends. The opal rested against her chest in the darkness. As I left, I turned up the flame on the lamp. And when I passed the door, I took the rifle.

*

With what was left of the night, I drove back to Shkin. Inside the cab of Mr Jack's HiLux, an artificial sweetness hung heavily in the air. From the rearview mirror, a bushel of cardboard air fresheners dangled, each one cut in the shape of a pine. To me they didn't smell like pine, but perhaps they had to Mr Jack. Also in the cab of his HiLux were the seat belts Atal didn't have in his truck. I buckled mine. At first it seemed a foolish precaution, but belted to my seat, breathing the sweet chemical smell of freshened air, I felt protected from the familiar world outside. There was power in such a feeling. With one hand on the steering wheel and the other holding the night-vision goggles, I found the north road, climbing and descending its many switchbacks. And from the clean cab, it seemed nothing could harm me, and with this feeling, it seemed the entire mountain range became like a knot untangled.

I passed over the worn lip of Qiam's crater. Gently, it crumbled beneath me. I continued and then, in the green distance of my night vision, I saw the outline of one of the Special Lashkar's trucks, a checkpoint. It was fixed to the mountainside like an ancient boulder, its power in its stillness. The truck's machine gunner slumped in the bed. As I drove towards him, he stirred and picked up his goggles, looking towards me. Then he slumped back into the bed. He had no intention of stopping Mr Jack's HiLux.

I rushed along the road, exhausted by the night's events. A great tiredness stirred in the back of my legs, running up my spine, blanketing my shoulders. I leaned over the steering wheel, pressed the goggles to my face, and willed myself to drive. I continued parallel to a stream that ran through the ravine towards Shkin. The water rolled out before me like a black ribbon, but soon it swam with morning light. Sunlit reds, greens from the pines, and the dark browns of everything else became increasingly clear. I dropped my goggles and stared straight ahead, towards the mountains that now shouldered the day's early glow.

As my HiLux heaved itself up a final climb, the firebase revealed itself – grubby, brown, and spread low. As I travelled this last stretch of road, a man leaned casually on a small motorbike several hundred yards outside the gate. He was handsomely dressed, conspicuous. A dark blue shalwar kameez hung to his knees with baggy trousers to match. On his head a grey, almost silver, turban was stacked in a neat bundle and its tail draped lazily over his shoulder and down his chest. He played with its end.

The man stepped into my path with his arm outstretched, demanding I stop. I pressed firmly on the brakes and as the weight of my HiLux shifted forwards, I saw it was Commander Sabir. He strolled towards my door with the unhurried elegance of all great predators.

The American's truck? he asked, sticking his head into my window.

He was at the meeting, I said. It was unplanned.

Commander Sabir nodded, licked his exposed lower gums with the underside of his tongue, absorbing what such a thing meant. And it is done? he asked.

Yes, Atal, Gazan, and Mr Jack, I said.

Mr Jack, he spoke the name, letting go of something once familiar. And you are certain about Atal?

Not wanting to speak his name again, I nodded.

Good, he said. Things will be different now, Aziz.

There will be no peace, I answered.

War is a mother to men such as us, he replied. It is a mother whose generosity brought you badal and will bring me my outpost. Men who forget about her generosity wind up like the three you just left.

What remains for me? I asked.

Plenty, if you choose. But you can't come to Shkin anymore. You are completely outside us now. But with this, you are valuable. Gazan is gone, but someone must lead his fighters. You.

I am not Gazan, I spit back.

No, you're not, he replied. You're not a fool as he was, and we will be better for it. He settled his stare on mine, and his logic trickled neatly down to an unquestionable conclusion that chilled the space between us.

And my brother?

He'll be cared for just as he's always been, said Commander Sabir.

No, I told him. I want to see my brother.

Very well, see him, he offered, waving his hand limply, as if he were giving me a trifle. Drive on to Orgun. I'll make the arrangements.

I pressed him: And after?

Return to Atal's home and wait. Gazan's fighters will find you soon enough. I will see to it.

I understood, but I wanted to hear him say what I understood and asked: What will I do with them then?

You'll lead them and they'll follow, he answered. They'll follow whoever clothes them, feeds them, and arms them. I do all of this and you will do all this through me.

And what of us, you and me?

We'll serve the war, he replied. And we'll prosper.

Give me time to consider this. First, I will go to Orgun to see my brother, and if I accept, I'll send you a message from Atal's home.

Of course, said Commander Sabir. Only if you accept.

*

I set out towards Orgun, and the north road ran flat and straight across the high desert plain. I began my journey without sleep and felt like a trespasser from yesterday.

I drove for hours. My only interruption was the sun, bearing down on the horizon. It set and the road became crowded in the darkness. Truck drivers, their workday finished, squatted along the shoulder fixing dinner. I thought of the young Mumtaz, with his father, doing the same. I wondered if tonight he prepared dinner for me in case I decided to return. I knew he wondered about what choices I'd made since leaving. At some point he'd learn of those choices. This made me want never to see him again.

A smattering of lights lined the horizon. Orgun. Soon the dust of the plain yielded to farmers' fields that were rutted and hard, waiting for crops. Among the fields were clusters of mud huts that made up the outskirts of the city. I continued to drive and Orgun rose up and swallowed me. Green, red, and blue shopfronts lined the streets. Small cooking fires glowed from within. Out front, merchants sat in circles, speaking beneath painted signs with scripts twisted into calligraphy, advertising the products in their stores. But sitting in this way was no longer for me. I was now a passerby to the evening's rituals and their civility.

I pulled up next to the shabby two-storey hospital. An ambulance was parked on the street outside. I left the black HiLux beside it. Exhausted and stiff, I approached the front entrance's light blue double doors, where a red sickle moon had been added since I'd left last winter – soon it'd be fall. The fresh paint had seeped into the chipped bottom layers, leaving the sickle moon with an uneven coat. I paused before entering and gathered a bit of strength for this final part of my journey. I didn't know what I'd feel when I found my brother, but this last day had left me numb and I wasn't sure I'd feel anything.

I entered the hospital and its wide linoleum corridor was empty. I remembered the surgeons rushing down it after the bombing, and my desperation, and my brother, gazing up at me, slipping. Halfway down the corridor was the operating room where he'd first been taken. I swung open its double doors, wondering if a similar scene would greet me. Inside were ten beds in two rows of five, each with crisp sheets, and next to them surgical tools laid on small-wheeled stands, clean, and ready for the cutting. A freshly shaven man in blue scrubs, a doctor perhaps, fiddled over one of the beds.

Is there someone you're looking for? he asked without glancing up.

No, I said. I'm just waiting.

Well, you can't wait in here, he replied. Wait outside.

That's what I'd done before, waited outside. I lacked the energy to find my brother with what remained of the night. I stepped into the corridor and sat on the freshly buffed floor, my back to the wall. I tucked my legs into my chest, the sharp smell of bleach and other chemicals rising to my nose. The floor's smooth hardness was uncomfortable, but its cleanness was a luxury. I laid my head between my arms and fell asleep.

★

There was a soft tapping at my foot. I looked up and rails of white burning bulbs ran down the ceiling. A lean, hard silhouette broke up the light.

Get off the ground, Aziz.

It was Taqbir, still trolling the hallways in his neatly pressed uniform, just as I'd first met him. He offered me his hand. I grasped it, thick and strong compared to mine. He pulled me up.

You look well, I said.

You look tired, he replied, the same as when I first met you. Commander Sabir told me you'd soon arrive. He said I needed to be ready to greet you. It seems you are a very important man now.

His smile was equal parts warmth and contempt.

My brother? I asked.

He's doing well, said Taqbir. Come.

He escorted me down the long linoleum hallway until we reached a corner room at its end.

Ali's in there and quite comfortable, he said with some pride.

He's no longer in the tent with the others?

Of course not, replied Taqbir. We care for our own.

He swung open the door.

Take your time, he said. I'll be just outside.

The room was too big for Ali. He lay in its far corner in a bed by the window, his head turned, looking through it, his face stubbled and hollow. A light blue hospital gown hung cleanly from his shoulders. His linen was fresh, but beneath his left side I could see that the flatness now rose all the way up to the hip. No one told me they'd taken more of the leg, and I thought of Ali being cut on alone. The stump that remained stuck out from beneath his sheets, as black and rotted as a winter log left in the snow. On a table by the door, flowers were clustered in two crystal jars.

I shut the door behind me. His dead stare continued out the window. I walked towards his bedside. There was no chair in the room for a visitor, so I knelt and grasped his palm. Through my thumb, I felt the tendons on the back of his hand and they were delicate as bird bones. I could feel where each one fused with his wrist. The muscle covering those connections had starved.

You are well, Aziz? he whispered in a rasp.

I am. And you? My question seemed ridiculous.

I am better since they moved me, he replied.

I didn't want to ask when he'd been moved. I assumed it was once I'd become indispensable to Commander Sabir. We sat together for some time. He gazed out the window. I rested my head on his bedside and shut my eyes. Once again exhaustion rolled over me, but I didn't sleep. I lay there with my brother and held on to the past I'd always known, the one in which he'd cared for me. Then, breaking the stillness, he draped a weak hand across my shoulder. You must work very hard to keep me here, he said. I imagine you've prospered and made a life for yourself, yes? Have you started some business? Have you? Your education, it has served you well, has it not?

It has, I said.

Yes, he said, whatever business you're in must be doing well for me to get this treatment.

It is, I said quietly.

Ali looked past me towards the back of the room. Taqbir opened the door a crack to check on us. His green uniform was framed against the white walls of the hospital. Ali shut his eyes and looked away from him.

Tell me how you've prospered, my brother asked.

He didn't want to hear of badal. He wanted to hear about a life I could never have. I smiled and made a last deceit for him.

I'm apprenticed to a good man in Kabul, I said. That is why it is difficult for me to visit.

Ah, replied Ali, his voice scratching. No apologies. But tell me, what does this man do?

He is a great merchant, I answered. He has a trucking business.

Trucking. He breathed the word as though it were a prayer. This is a fine business and steady work.

Yes, I said. I have a knack for it.

That's good, replied Ali. You always learned quick, Brother.

I continued: Yes and I've received a promotion.

In such a short time? What a thing.

With my promotion, my boss gave me some vacation to see you, I said.

It seems you are an important man now, said Ali.

Perhaps, I answered.

Your boss sounds very generous, he said. You must thank him for me.

I held his one hand between my two as I spoke: I will, Ali, of course I will.

Good, he replied. Now I must rest. I'm not strong as I used to be.

His admission made my throat turn thick. I told him: I know, Brother.

You'll come visit again soon?

Of course, I said, and of them all, this was my worst lie.

Ali looked back at me and offered a smile with his thin lips. Then he let go of my hand and rolled his head towards the window. He stared outside and his face changed. Once again it was empty.

IV

I STAND ON THE LIP OF A WADI, looking north. My HiLux is parked in the empty streambed below. The moon reflects off its dark paint. It is a horned moon, carved down to its ends. Across the high plain, tucked among the foothills, is FOB Sharana. At night, its towers are all that can be seen. The Americans wall themselves in with a ring of lights. While everyone sleeps, only they run their generators.

I climb down from the lip of the wadi. The moon casts thin shadows in the dry streambed. Here the earth breaks easily and is covered by stones. I kick it up as I go. My steps release the wet smell of old floods, a reminder that violent waters often pass through here, sweeping away all but the strongest stones.

But always it becomes dry again.

I pull a wool blanket over my shoulders and lie across the backseat of the HiLux. I shut my eyes.

I imagine what it's like behind their walls. There will be an American there who debriefs Afghans. This I've heard. I'll ask for him. I'll tell him he has a problem, that he's lost control. Mr Jack had wanted to work with Gazan, to control him, now I've become Gazan. When I return to Gomal, Commander Sabir will ensure that I am armed from funds their government pays him for the Special Lashkar. I will be the leverage Commander Sabir uses against the village to get his outpost built. The Americans influence none of this. I'll offer them my help, but they have two things I want, two things Sabir can't give me.

Without anyone to care for her, Fareeda will die. I will ask them for the medicine Mr Jack once gave Atal. He purposed his life to care for hers. Now I have done the same. I will return to Gomal and lead Gazan's men so she might live.

And with the Americans' help, I'll get rid of Sabir. I'll replace him. With his position, I'll prosper in the war and succeed where Gazan and Atal failed. I'll take enough to someday leave it, and bring with me those I love.

Thinking of all I can offer the Americans, I find sleep. I am filthy and cold, alone in the wadi.

Then, with the first light of the morning, I am again awake, surrounded by the smell of the wet and violent earth.

It has begun to rain.

I crouch among the stones. Between them, water pools. I wash my hands and face in it.

ACKNOWLEDGEMENTS

This novel is dedicated to two Afghan soldiers who, consumed by their war, will likely never have a chance to read it. My hope is that the book proves a worthy acknowledgement to the world they lived in and the war they fought

My gratitude to Dick Snyder, a stalwart mentor to whom I am indebted.

I am blessed to have PJ Mark as an agent and friend.

Marya Spence provided a second set of eyes on everything, there's none sharper.

Liese Mayer and Paul Whitlatch at Scribner made this book better, and believed in it. I couldn't ask for more thoughtful and talented partners.

Lea Carpenter and Judy Sternlight read early drafts, and both proved generous with their time and insight.

And my family, who've always supported me, but particularly my mother, a novelist herself, who taught me to tell stories on the sofa in her office, and my wife, Xanthe, who always believed, both when it was easy, but especially when it was hard.